Praise for *Losing Francis*

"Robert F. Sommer's book of essays, *Losing Francis*, offers a unique and urgent contribution to the literature of the Bush wars. After deployments to Iraq and Afghanistan, Sommer's son battled hearing loss, kidney damage, and a deep sense of moral unease about his war experiences, before dying in a car accident. This powerful recounting of one veteran's life doubles as a history of the Bush era, told by a watchful father, torn between love for his son and distrust of the wars he's been sent to fight. Both harrowing and lovely, *Losing Francis* is a vibrant, indispensable document of life in our time."
— Whitney Terrell, author of *The Good Lieutenant*

"A poignant account of one couple's journey through the shadow cast by the death of their son. Inextricably woven into the story is the nefarious reality of the nation's ruinous recent wars. A compelling and insightful book."
— Mark Karlin, Editor, *BuzzFlash at Truthout*

"Robert F. Sommer's *Losing Francis: Essays on the Wars at Home* is a powerful meditation on grief and memory that centers around the loss of his son: a troubled youth, a decorated soldier, and a struggling veteran, who, like so many veterans of the recent wars, finds re-entry into civilian life a challenge he could not overcome. Sommer's prose often rises to the poetic, his storytelling is poignant yet never sentimental, and his unflinching honesty in relating his son's life and death leave the reader with a lump in the throat and a righteous anger. *Losing Francis* will surely take its

earned place in the lamentably-large library of great literature of the home front."

— Jeanetta Calhoun Mish, Oklahoma State Poet Laureate 2017-18, author of *What I Learned at the War*

"*Losing Francis* is a father's loving elegy-in-essays about a combat veteran son who survived the worst in Afghanistan and Iraq, but who could not expiate what he had seen and done afterwards. What hope did his son have, Robert F. Sommer asks, in an America that seems incurious about its own wars and that prefers lip-service to empathy? *Losing Francis* is a lyrical indictment of the historical, political, and cultural forces that keep America at war, and then leave its veterans out in the cold. It also models a way forward. If the United States it is to live up to its best self, if it is to become a supportive home to its veterans, it must find the strength to be honest about the foreign and American lives its wars destroy. Robert F. Sommer shows us how."

— Max Rayneard, *The Telling Project*

"Robert F. Sommer has written a remarkably compelling book with boldness and startling passion. He shows us that even after the last troop comes home, war is never over. *Losing Francis* recounts his story about the short-circuiting of the life of his son with eloquence and insight, but most of all, with astonishing courage. It reverberates and teaches and beyond all else, it rings with hope."

— Barry Sanders, author of *The Green Zone: The Environmental Costs of Militarism*

"In *Losing Francis: Essays on the Wars at Home*, Robert F. Sommer captures the realities of war and its effects both on soldiers and their parents, who deal with so much they can't control, including sometimes the loss of a child. This is first-rate, thoughtful writing that will move any reader."

– Maryfrances Wagner, Thorpe Menn
Literary Excellence Award recipient for
Red Silk and co-editor of *I-70 Review*

"*Losing Francis: Essays on the Wars at Home* is a must read for all Americans, but as author Robert F. Sommer himself concedes, most Americans, dawdling over trivial engagements and personal comforts, have only fleeting interest in America's involvement in wars fought in far places or the men and women sent there to fight, suffer, and die. That leaves those of us who have experienced war, directly or indirectly, to reflect on Sommer's experiences of dealing with the post-discharge loss of his son in a war that was, and continues to be, at best, ill-conceived.

"Sommer's syntax is at once scholarly and lyrical – and his message heartbreaking. He will make you angry at a government that spends weeks training soldiers to kill and go to war, only to let them fend for themselves when they come home. In his search for the truth about his son's deployments, he writes, 'I too had become an actor in a play I didn't write.... Participation was not an option.'"

– H. C. Palmer, author of *Feet of the Messenger*

"In *Losing Francis*, Sommer renders the ongoingness of loss – a process without end but with certain key beginning and mutation points. It is an indictment of our national tolerance for the casualties of war and a probing act of devotion in which absences (of a child, of a nation's sense of its own culpability) are made palpable through the small moments and consequential events that lead up to, surround, and define their shifting borders."

– Elizabeth Witte, Associate Editor, *The Common*
and Director, *The Common* in the Classroom

"*Losing Francis* is a word-guided tour through different worlds collapsing into each other, some wanted most not. It is the story of a son and parents thrown into the worlds of war and death, buddies and enemies, hope and anguish. That most feared news then comes not from the foreign fields but from highway police in the middle of the night. This painful tour challenges beliefs from all sides – those looking for growth in the military, those who look down on joiners, those who supported the wars, and those parents who hope. In the end there are no convenient lessons, only the tours of realities that one hopes will at least give pause. Too important to miss."

– Michael McDermott, Co-founder and
Director Black Earth Institute

Praise for *A Great Fullness* (a novel)
2017 Thorpe Menn Literary Excellence Award Nominee

"Sommer has crafted a compelling story of fine character sketches …."
– *Wichita Eagle*

"As in a Greek tragedy, a horrific death occurs off-stage in Bob Sommer's second novel, *A Great Fullness*, and colors every visible moment of this suspenseful story about a surviving child. Loss weaves through the fabric of every life in this wise parable."

— Denise Low, Kansas Poet Laureate, 2007-2009,
author of *Ghost Stories of the New West*

"With cinematic clarity and pace, *A Great Fullness* takes us inside a family caught in turmoil, as the drama of their lives reflects our troubled society and its broken capacity for joy. With illuminating skill Bob Sommer heightens the reader's awareness of both family dysfunction and our nation's drift into war and ecological disaster ... while weaving humor and insight into an entertaining and relevant five-star tale."

— David Ray, author of *Sam's Book*
and *Gathering Firewood*

"Bob Sommer writes eloquently about ordinary Midwestern Americans confronted with the extraordinarily disruptive pressures of the twenty-first century. Again and again in this story of a girl raised by her aunt and uncle after her home has dissolved in a flurry of domestic bloodletting, one is struck with the complexity of seemingly nondescript characters and the menace behind the bland appearance of bedroom communities and sleek suburban malls. One is asked to care deeply about each character, likeable and not, and to experience an astonishing degree of secret sharing with respect to hopes, plans, perplexities, vulnerabilities, and defeats. The Kansas of *A Great Fullness* is too deeply understood and too particularly and painfully rendered to be just any place. Readers will come away from this book with a deepened understanding of the violence and longing that shape contemporary American life."

— William Merrill Decker, author of
Kodak Elegy: A Cold War Childhood

"In this sensitive and heart-felt novel Bob Sommer examines the impact of shattering violence on three generations of an American family. While rooted in the specific landscape of eastern Kansas in the late twentieth century, the story opens itself to all of us, tracing with care and insight the struggle to overcome loss and to forge new bonds of love and trust in the face of all the challenges that life presents."

— Kimball Smith, author of *Missing Persons* and *Nothing Disappears*

Praise for *Where the Wind Blew* (a novel)

"This blistering, fast-paced tale of a man whose radical past catches up with him... cross-examines our culture, then and now."

— *Chronogram*

"*Where the Wind Blew* is a story of the past and an allegory of the present.... Bob Sommer hears the music and voices of the past and gives you what America has become today."

— Mason Williams (of "Classical Gas" fame)

"I found *Where the Wind Blew* engrossing and heartfelt....

Emotionally taut and historically intriguing, this novel explores the psyche of a man whose past finally catches him. Although set in the past, its themes transcend time."

– Ron Jacobs, author of *The Way the Wind Blew: A History of the Weather Underground*

"I had a hard time putting *Where the Wind Blew* down."

– Robert Pardun, author of *Prairie Radical: A Journey through the Sixties*

"... *Where the Wind Blew* is not intended to be a story about a hero but a parable of regret, and those stories are truest when the protagonists are people like us, ordinary people who are neither excessively virtuous nor intrinsically evil."

– *American Book Review*

"This story is so believable and well-told that I felt I had an insider's knowledge of what it would have been like to live through the protests on college campuses during the Vietnam War era."

– *Whistling Shade*

"... a masterful job of evoking memories of the halcyon days of political activism."

– *The Baby Boomer Brief*

Also by Robert F. Sommer

A Great Fullness

Where the Wind Blew

LOSING FRANCIS

Essays on the Wars at Home

Robert F. Sommer

Fomite
Burlington, VT

2018 © by Robert F. Sommer

Versions of several essays in this book have previously appeared, as follows:

"The Art of Grief: 'Windows and Mirrors,'" *The Common Online, July 14, 2017.*
"We Were Goats," *Red Earth Review,* Vol. 4, 2016.
"Bread Crumbs and Hatchet Marks," *O-Dark-Thirty,* Vol. 4, No. 1, 2015.
"Rust on the Hillsides," *Emrys Journal,* Vol. 33, 2015.
"Remedial Army," *New Plains Review,* Spring 2014.
"Leavenworth," *Rathalla Review,* Vol. 1, No. 3, Fall 2013; and *Rathalla Review 2014. Annual Anthology.* Named a "Notable Essay" in *The Best American Essays 2015.*
"On Line at the Post Office," *The Whirlybird Anthology of Kansas City Writers,* Whirlybird Press, 2012.
"No, We're Not from Texas," *Prick of the Spindle: A Quarterly Online Journal of the Literary Arts,* Vol. 2, No. 2, June 2008.

Cover image thanks to Pixabay user cocoparisienne, who made the image freely available for commercial uses such as book covers under Creative Commons License CC0.
https://pixabay.com/en/walkers-autumn-fog-man-human-mood-486583/

ISBN-13: 978-1-944388-46-1
Library of Congress Control Number: 2017964716

Fomite
58 Peru Street
Burlington, VT 05401
www.fomitepress.com

For you, Francis, with love

Contents

Prologue 1
Leavenworth 13
Remedial Army 33
American Soldier 61
On Line at the Post Office 114
Off the Radar 118
'No, We're Not from Texas' 123
Homeland 138
Rust on the Hillsides 173
Bread Crumbs and Hatchet Marks 192
The Art of Grief: 'Windows and Mirrors' 208
We Were Goats 229
Epilogue 259
Acknowledgments 267
About the Author 271

*He rose and stood upright,
And gazed upon his native coast and wept,
And smote his thigh, and said in bitter grief: "Ah me!
what region am I in, among
What people? lawless, cruel, and unjust?
Or are they hospitable men, who fear
The gods?"*

> *The Odyssey of Homer, XIII, 244-50*
> *(trans. William Cullen Bryant)*

*But where will they take
their grief, those who return from
distant battlefields?*

> —David Ray

I did not choose the stories; they chose me.
> —Eduardo Galleano
> *(Democracy Now!, May 8, 2013)*

Prologue

We lost Francis in the early hours of February 11, 2011, when he passed out at the wheel of his car and struck a utility pole. His blood-alcohol level was three times the legal limit. He was alone, and while no one else was hurt or killed, we are sometimes haunted by the thought that other lives also might have been lost in this tragedy. At twenty-seven years old, he was an Army veteran with tours in Iraq and Afghanistan behind him. In the three years since leaving the service, he'd become a fine chef and was just a few months from completing his culinary arts degree. Above all, he was our beloved son and brother. Our sorrow is deep and profound, and we will always live with it.

While every grieving family, to paraphrase Tolstoy, may grieve in its own way, our tragedy is not unique. Change a few details and the above paragraph might easily describe thousands of veterans and the sorrow with which their families live. A veteran of Iraq and Afghanistan is far more likely to die in a car wreck than the average American. Drug and alcohol abuse is widespread and dangerous behaviors commonplace, all of which fall on the infinite spectrum of unintended consequences from these wars – if any consequences of a war can truly be said to be unintended. Over 40 percent of returning veterans have been formally diagnosed with post-traumatic stress disorder, including Francis, with suicides reaching an epidemic scale.

In little more than whispers and fragmented sentences, we wondered at times, Heather and I did, in the early weeks and months after Francis died, if he'd done this to himself. On his "Suicide Risk Assessment" from the Kansas City VA, he offered a monosyllabic "Yes" in response to the question of whether he was "feeling depressed or hopeless," but "No" regarding whether he "had thoughts about death or about killing yourself." But we're parents, not case managers, and knew how fragile that No was. He'd been in treatment at the VA for PTSD, depression, chronic back and hip pain, and for substance abuse, mostly alcohol and marijuana. At various times, his meds included Trazodone, Naltrexone, Sertraline HCL, Zolpidem Tartrate, and Folic Acid – anti-depressants, drug abuse deterrents, sedatives, and the Folic Acid, usually prescribed for pregnant women or the anemic. The meds made him sick or agitated, or both, so he took them erratically, if at all. Or he just wanted to drink and knew they'd either make him really sick or kill him if he did both. The last doctor he saw told him his liver was shot and if he kept drinking it would kill him. Innumerable firefights and mortar shells had also left him with a 60 percent hearing loss in one ear and partial loss in the other. Tests at the VA further revealed cognitive impairment. He sometimes couldn't recall basic vocabulary words in normal conversation. But booze had become the wall that surrounded and imprisoned him, and us, wherever we turned to face all of the other obstacles lay beyond it.

"I want to feel revitalized," he said on his treatment plan.

Re-vitalized. Not a new life, but the recovery of a life that once had purpose, meaning, spirit, or so he believed, or wanted to believe. And perhaps, too, he couldn't decide if the life he was remembering or imagining was before the Army or in it. Like many other young men and women, he enlisted after hitting a dead end. We caught glimpses of that new vitality when he was in basic training at Fort Benning. But in later years, especially after he returned home, he knew that something had been lost, and also that he'd gotten lost searching for it. He was damaged, felt damaged, believed himself damaged. Civilian friends from the past, he said, did not understand. The wars were not part of their lives and had nothing to do with them. A couple of his friends told us later, after we lost him – almost as if confessing – that they had not understood until now. They had known him in a time before the Army, before the deployments, before he learned to kill other human beings, before he watched friends die, before he wondered if a child reaching for candy might be concealing a weapon, before he saw the devastation and chaos and resentment of two countries invaded and occupied by the U.S., before the Army and the wars, and maybe even before he tumbled into the rabbit hole that led him to think he had no options left but to join the Army, and then the despair from what these wars had done to him. Becoming revitalized was how he capsulized the longing for a hazy nostalgia, paradoxically, for a future of, not pleasure, but joy. They are distinct: pleasure is an alcohol-fueled tailgate party at Arrowhead Stadium; joy is falling in love, having a purpose, feeling needed. These experiences, he believed, were passing him by. He was, he also wrote on his treatment plan, a "good family member" and a "caring" individual. Despite all, we knew the depth of truth in these descriptors.

But the booze had gotten so bad by the fall of 2010, three years after he left the Army, that he checked himself into the VA for six weeks of in-patient rehab. The program cleared out his system for a short spell, but he was soon drinking again. Some evenings he'd say he was going to an AA meeting and come home hours later in a cloud of bar-room odors. One morning, freshly showered and shaved, he burst into my office, feeling great, he said: he'd been dry for ten days! He was finally on track. That night he celebrated by getting drunk and crashing at whosever apartment he'd landed, which in turn only led to another bout of depression. Some mornings I'd find empty bottles barely "hidden" behind the sofa in the family room, as if left there to be found, and burned up aluminum foil pipes on the coffee table, as troubling as fire hazards as they were as so much more evidence of the sorry state into which he'd fallen. He stashed empties in his closet by the dozen, which more than once we told him to clean out, or sometimes did so ourselves when he wasn't home, a quiet gesture of support, or resolve, offering, we hoped, yet another fresh start, or deluding ourselves into believing it was. But he always seemed to stumble out of the blocks. On the morning of the day he died, I was angry with him and he knew it. The drinking, the drinking and driving, the drinking and passing out on the sofa, the drinking altogether and how bad it'd gotten. We avoided each other as he left the house. I was

Prologue

in the kitchen, where I'd just found a stray beer bottle cap on the counter. I heard him leave but didn't call goodbye. I caught a partial glimpse of him as he was halfway out the door. The last time I saw him alive, the last chance I'd ever have to speak with him.

There was no indication he was depressed that night. Heather called him around 10:00 p.m., before he left work at the restaurant, a nightly ritual to get him through the next hour, to make sure he was coming straight home. At least get him here. Get him through one more night. Drive home sober. Get here safely, whatever he may do next as we slept – the little we slept in those days. The calls usually lasted just a minute or two: I'm okay. I'm on the way home. And, that night, I love you. Not part of the script, but it didn't seem to have any special subtext either. This had become one of his responses to the wars, to deployment, to coming home: affection, saying I love you without prompting. He loved her; he loved us and his family, in spite of it all. He never got angry with us in all that time. Never threatened us or flew into a rage at home. The bedrock of his spirit was fractured with stress and worry and guilt, even as waves of happiness and his perfect-pitch wit would sometimes sweep into our lives like the sweet whisper of a breeze straining through pine branches and shaking cottonwood leaves in the fall. It warmed her that night. We read for a while, turned out the lights, went to sleep. Or she did.

I knew, with some annoyance, that soon after I drifted off his car would buzz into the driveway and the door lock would beep, punctuating his arrival and jolting me out of sleep. But he wasn't on the way home. He went out to a bar with friends until sometime after 1:00 a.m. At 3:00 a.m. there was a heavy persistent knocking at the door. Two police officers on the walkway, two squad cars idling in the street.

For a while we parried questions from relatives and friends about what happened, why his car suddenly ran off the road. He'd worked late, we said. He was tired and fell asleep at the wheel. Others may have drawn their own conclusions, but who's going to argue with grieving parents? If we felt any personal shame about knowing the truth, it was outweighed by the instinct to protect him so he wouldn't be remembered for dying drunk behind the wheel. You can't really call it an accident when someone dies this way. There's blame, fault, resonance. It threatens to consume both tragedy and memory – to displace the life story of the unique and special person we'd lost.

Tragedies like ours unfold quietly. They flit past in Web links and news ledes and disappear into the ether of media chaos. Francis's death was summed up in a thirty-second TV report. Rush hour traffic had backed up on the highway because of the wreck. Another headline, another tragedy. A week later, on the morning of his wake, I was blindsided in the barber shop. Numb, speechless, still in shock, I'd taken up the paper not to read but to screen myself from the chatter that surrounded me – and there he was: his name, a little black-and-white flag icon, the obituary I'd already forgotten writing a week earlier. I sat like a zombie, reading it over and over, inhumed in a dense, suffocating cloud that pressed and squeezed me from all sides. The voices in the room grew distant, like murmurs from across a chasm or field. I pressed my lips shut to hold back the deep wail that would have erupted if someone had even spoken to me at that moment. A lifetime of haircuts took me through the ritual that followed without the need to utter more than a few syllables. The barber sensed that something wasn't right, but he let me be and chattered with the men lounging in waiting chairs, clipping as if I were an overgrown hedge. The paper sat where I left it. Another customer would soon take it up and scan basketball scores or scoff at an editorial. Francis would disappear into the back pages, as invisible now as he'd been while he was deployed and later, as he navigated the alien world of home, scarred with invisible wounds and moral injuries from the wars.

This recognition was not an epiphany of that moment, but rather confirmation of an awareness that had plagued us, Heather and me, for years. The 9/11 attacks, the initial entries into Afghanistan in October 2001 and Iraq in March 2003 had drawn widespread attention, but Americans soon lost interest. The wars slogged on. Nine-Eleven became a kind of sacramental memory, with rituals and reverence to commemorate the events of that day, the tragedies, but notably lacking in self-reflection. The American war machine had been stoked up. Militarism took on a life of its own, justified by a widespread sense of American victimhood. The world was given notice: We had been attacked, and you were either with us or against us. Yet even this fever soon broke. Americans grew bored. The mantras of terrorism and vigilance became embedded in the foundation of post-9/11 culture, but like the foundation of a house, only got attention when there was a crack or leak – or the Administration needed to distract citizens from the creeping escalation of the wars. Which otherwise slid off the grand radar screen of our collective vision, displaced by constellations of small screens, and large, which we filled with games and texts and pictures of dinner plates and dogs and ourselves, eating, doing tricks, cheering on our teams and our tribes, and maligning those of other tribes with all of invective and bile our emojis and keyboard shorthand could bring to our tribal skirmishes. Consumption became a competitive sport, and war was colored in sacerdotal shades in those rare moments when it passed through our lives, but it mostly had no lasting impact because it affected so few in all but momentary ways. I have no doubt that had I shared my grief in the barber shop that day, it would have drawn great sympathy – and I should not so glibly fault the men there for not giving what they would have given freely – but rather, what I was observing in the clarity of those hyper-emotional moments was the life that existed beyond the world of war and its costs and consequences. Most of the essays in this book in some way draw on that theme.

To be sure, our tragedy is not measurable against the immense, now-generational, suffering of Iraqis and Afghans who have been most oppressed by these wars, or the millions of Middle Eastern refugees displaced by their spillover. Nor is my intention to drape us in victimhood. Rather, it is to share a handful of episodes in the story of our wanderings through the years of these wars and to describe how we experienced them in a world that was distant from the one that surrounded us – even though it was that other world that assented to war and, whether actively or (mostly) passively, approved and supported it. And even within our world was (and is) the remote country of dissenters to war that we occupied.

Prologue

Being a military family is sometimes thought to mean that you're "pro-war," that you want to go to war, that maybe you even like war, or at least that you unquestionably support war when the country is at war. But that was not us – and such stereotypes are unfair even to some of the most hawkish of military families. As I'll describe in one essay, more than a few high-ranking military officers were among the most vocal opponents of the Iraq invasion. More to the point of our experience is the overriding question of how you support a loved one – and all of the men and women he's with – who is at war while opposing the war itself. This conundrum is not new in history, nor simple to resolve. This book is, in part, an attempt to explore the uncomfortable need to balance and negotiate these conflicting feelings.

If the story of our journey were linear, it would form a circle. But the experience was anything but story-like. It doesn't form a complete and satisfying narrative, with all of the necessary elements of drama, from exposition to climax and denouement. Rather it felt multi- (or even extra-) dimensional, as if we had bounced about in an undefined yet enclosed space, where we suddenly found ourselves in unfamiliar landscapes and then recognized them as places we'd already been, though in dreamlike ways now reshaped with new features and inhabitants. The tragic and awful finality of Francis's life was also, we discovered, a beginning of sorts. So I begin at that end-beginning with a meditation on the site of the national cemetery where Francis's remains rest, a story itself that took me back to long before it was a national cemetery or Kansas or even a territory in the young nation. How it's an ending is obvious; how it became a beginning was our discovery of what our lives would become after losing Francis. The essays that follow trace our journey from boot camp to his deployments to Iraq and Afghanistan and his return home. The final pieces close the circle with a meditation on art and grief and the Afghan victims of that war, followed by a visit to Francis's Army friend Bobby, who welcomed me into his world and offered glimpses of Francis and their experiences in Afghanistan in ways I had not imagined.

In calling this book *Losing Francis* I mean to suggest more than our loss of a son and brother. He lost himself in the wars, too. And when he came home we found ourselves in a new battle to save him from his own guilt and sorrow. He may have been discharged from the Army, but the wars still raged within him and we found ourselves in the fight too.

Overland Park, June 16, 2017

I have no words for this. It keeps coming back in waves. There's a moment before waking when it's not there, but I know something is there and I'm afraid of it, and then it comes to me and I'm awake and the day begins with no return to sleep. Then the waves come throughout the day.

— *My journal entry for Tuesday, February 15, 2011, four days after we lost Francis.*

Leavenworth

WE ARE GLIDING OVER the smooth pavement of a lonely cemetery lane with the car windows open when a ruckus erupts in a grove of oak trees. It's near dusk and the grounds are mostly deserted. Just Heather and I in the car. No one else around.

One of the collective nouns for squirrels is scurry. That's what it is – a scurry of squirrels, chattering and barking.

In their midst, on the grass, a red-tailed hawk with a bloodied beak clutches a limp gray body in his talons. I stop and shut off the engine and we watch. The squirrels chatter frantically, trying to drive the hawk away. But he (if it is a he) coolly stays put, unthreatened, indifferent to the clamor, likely resting from the kill. Then, abruptly, he spreads his wings and leaps into the air with his quarry. The squirrels quiet and linger for a moment, until, one by one, they skitter off into the canopy or onto the ground to forage for acorns.

This deadly encounter would have passed without human notice if we hadn't happened by just then. The distant white noise of nature, which often seems playful or joyous to our ears, is mostly the sound of turf battles and fear, of life and death. The history of our nonhuman fellow travelers is unwritten, unrecorded in their own ranks; their deaths uncommemorated, their battles untold. It's tempting to imagine some imprint of loss lingering in the squirrels' collective memory in that moment before they resumed the work of survival. More likely they were waiting until the shock of the encounter faded and it was safe to return to their business.

We'd come here to Leavenworth National Cemetery to visit our son Francis, whose remains rest in Section 58A, on the north side of the cemetery. In real estate terms this section is "newer," platted but still unsettled. The few trees on the easy hillside are saplings, so there's no shade. Grass turf has recently been laid but is not complete. The ground is muddy after rain and snow, hard-packed when it's dry or cold. It will take on the manicured look of the rest of the cemetery in time, but that will require the sad business of occupancy to continue.

Friends of ours recently laid their son to rest nearby. His gravestone is now in place too, but the turf progress has yet to reach westward the dozen or so rows from Francis to his grave. Several rows to the east of Francis is the marker for a soldier who also served in his Army division. This troubled boy – he was barely more than a teenager – took his own life, as did our friends' son, two of many in the epidemic of suicides among Iraq and Afghanistan veterans. Along with Francis, they are nestled among veterans and casualties of Viet Nam, Korea, World War II, even a few soldiers from The Great War, as it was known before the twentieth century's great wars required numbering. We've begun to feel a kinship with a few of Francis's immediate neighbors, as if, being older, they might look out for him. An odd bond to form, one-sided, I realize, but still a comforting conceit, one of many unexpected sensations we've experienced in losing him.

Another is our connection to this place. Until we lost Francis we didn't know it was here, an admission I make with a dose of embarrassment because it's only thirty minutes from home. We'd passed the main gate at Fort Leavenworth, the Army post at the north end of town, many times. There's a cemetery there too, while Leavenworth National Cemetery, here at the southern edge of Leavenworth and just over the city line from Lansing, is a different venue. The two are easily confused.

This region is thick with historical and geographical points of interest. Across Muncie Road from the entry gates to the national cemetery, a double row of chain link fencing crowned with glittering concertina wire surrounds a cluster of unmarked warehouse-like buildings. Here inmates at Lansing State Penitentiary manufacture office furniture and other goods. Prison labor has progressed, if this is progress, a long way from stamping license plates. This prison has its own unique history, most notably including the execution of the infamous killers Truman Capote immortalized in his nonfiction novel *In Cold Blood*. Fortunately, the prison grounds slip quickly from view as you pass through the cemetery gate.

For many the word *Leavenworth* is synonymous with the storied federal prison, officially known as United States Penitentiary, Leavenworth. This is up at the north end of town, not far from the military post. With its massive stone facing and countless rows of barred windows, it could be the setting for a black-and-white James Cagney movie from the 1930s. It even looks black and white. Oddly, despite its fierce reputation (and appearance), it's now a medium-security prison, mostly because of age and the efficiencies of building new prisons elsewhere that incorporate the latest innovations in penal technology.

In our home *Leavenworth* is a metonym for the national cemetery. Other uses require a modifier: *the city of Leavenworth, Fort Leavenworth*. When Francis passed away we were offered a choice between the cemetery on the Army post or the national cemetery. In the fugue of grief we weren't certain what to do. It seemed like a distinction without a difference. But then we realized that national cemeteries are open to the public, while if we brought Francis onto the Army post, we – and our family and friends – would not be able to visit him without passing through a checkpoint. From past trips to Fort Benning and Fort Drum while he was in the service, we knew what that meant in the post-9/11 universe of the military – producing IDs and insurance cards, telling blank-faced soldiers clutching automatic weapons why we were here, possibly having the car searched (happened more than once). It wasn't difficult to imagine Heather sitting stoically beside me and enduring these exchanges until we were allowed to pass. Unlikely as it was, there was always a chance we'd be turned away. I would never approach the gate without anxiety or the infinitesimal fear that my reason for being there wouldn't be good enough on a given day. I imagined this haze of anticipation infecting our grief. We were so deeply immersed in grief in the days after we lost Francis that we had not begun to learn its shape and parameters, how it later becomes a kind of cloud or fog that surrounds you at times and then slides off into the distance, casting shadows on the horizon, but never out of sight and always likely to blow in again soon, and surprisingly, how welcome it is when it returns. At that moment, sitting at a polished walnut table with Heather and the funeral director, as insipid music in the key of sorrow drifted through the room like incense, I realized in some instinctive way that we would come to value our grief and that soldiers with weapons and low voltage suspicions would forever taint our visits. The future unfolded itself, not seen, but felt – the permanence of death, our commitment to wherever we took our son. The funeral director acknowledged that the national cemetery was the better choice. That's what it would be, though we'd never seen it and didn't know where it was.

It's been over two years since we brought Francis here. His services now seem like a wind-blown mirage. A gusty day, unseasonably warm for February in Kansas. His flag billowed and flapped as if resisting its role in the ceremony as the honor guard struggled to fold it. Salvos of blank rifle fire sent jolts through our gathering. When the first order was called, I sought Heather's hand as if to brace her, or maybe myself, for the shock – but nothing helps. We were as dazed as if we'd found ourselves on the moon. One of Francis's Army friends, Isaac, a staff sergeant in dress-blue with whom he'd served in Iraq and Afghanistan, retrieved a few spent cartridges from the grass and brought them to me later. A tradition or custom – I didn't know – one of many small gestures that became part of our initiation into this side of our lives. We'd now passed into a new place; everything about it was strange; the life we'd known was gone, or forever altered. Matt, the soldier who'd given his eulogy, lingered until the gathering dispersed and then walked up to Francis's urn in stiff, formal steps. His shoulders quaking, he saluted Francis, an image I still find so moving it's difficult to set down in words.

Our visits to the cemetery have evolved since then. The grounds are familiar. I've looked into its history too. Human activity in this region long predates the U.S. planting a flag in the Kansas territory – or anyone even calling it a territory. My friend Craig, who lives not far from here, showed me spearheads and other stone tools dating back thousands of years he found along a creek bed that runs through his property. He also lent me an old map of the tribal provenance of the region, but before I get into that I must share a few words about my son Francis, who brought us here.

He was twenty-seven when we lost him. His life began and ended in less than half the years I had lived by then. This is one of the many hard things about losing a child, reckoning the measure of your own life as it surrounds his. When he was born I had already been alive longer than the full length of the life he would live, and now I'm beginning to measure the interval since he died in years. Time becomes elastic and slippery in such calibrations. The mind wants a spatial or pictorial model to comprehend it. Instead, random images from that parenthesis of time, like thumbnail pictures in a digital folder of photos, swirl about chaotically, darting this way and that like minnows in pond water.

He'd been out of the Army three years when late one night – or rather, early one cold February morning – his car drifted off the road and struck a utility pole. He was alone, listening to "Here Comes the Sun" on his iPhone, and had been drinking. How Francis died is not counted among statistics about veterans. Studies have been done, to be sure. Veterans of Iraq and Afghanistan are known to drive recklessly and engage in dangerous behaviors. A veteran of these wars is 75 percent more likely to die in a car accident than most Americans. Drug and alcohol abuse are widespread among recent veterans. In this Francis is included in the statistics because he was treated for alcoholism by the VA. But whether tallied or not, stories like ours surround us, hidden within sight, driving past in other cars, pushing shopping carts in grocery stores, painting our homes, or, like Francis, preparing our food in a restaurant kitchen and filling a seat in a community college classroom. The manner and moment of death are not the defining elements of a life.

Francis enlisted at nineteen and became a civilian once again at twenty-four. Youth seems incongruous with being a veteran. It's easier to think of veterans as old men in VFW caps glittering with pins or tattooed, grizzled bikers with Viet Nam rockers on their vests. Of course, those vets were young once too. And now the Iraq and Afghanistan wars have flooded the country with hundreds of thousands of young vets like Francis. But his status as a veteran is frozen in youth. He will always be young. He is one of the youngest in the field where he rests. I have walked it and found myself compulsively doing the arithmetic of dates on headstones. There are no children in a military cemetery. The only soldier I've found younger than Francis is one of the suicides I mentioned earlier.

Francis was heavily decorated. He neatly arranged his medals and awards on a shelf in his room that remained undisturbed and uncluttered even as the bed went unmade, laundry piled up, fishing tackle and biking gear accumulated, and dust gathered on the awards. But stray clutter never landed on that shelf. He received Commander's Coins for eight separate missions in Afghanistan. He was awarded the Army Commendation Medal twice. He received top honors for a leadership training course at Fort Drum. The items on the shelf included a blue infantry pin with a cluster to indicate he'd been in battle, assorted ribbons and pins and dog tags, and a bullet he dug out of his boot after a firefight. Still, the display had a sorrowful look, and not only from the haze of dust that settled on it. His eyes went vacant when he talked about some of the items here, as if their purpose had been drained of meaning, as if they were honoring events too awful to remember and actions too banal, or atrocious, to be honored. They were meticulously arranged, but in a way that seemed utterly lonely. Only Heather and I and his brother Alex and sister Erin ever saw these medals. It wasn't until he was gone and I assembled everything into a display case for his wake that his friends and extended family saw them. He was surely proud of his honors, too – most had come after great hardship and much bloodletting and loss of life – but there was sadness, even guilt, in the way he assembled and spoke of them, as if these conflicting emotions swirled about in his conscience like oil and water, and the medals were there as much to remind him of one as the other.

He deployed to Iraq for a year and then to Afghanistan's notorious "valley of death," the Korengal Valley (*the corngall,* he'd say), for sixteen months. He rarely spoke about his deployments – almost never about the missions, the battles, the firefights, the killing. We caught random glimpses, like realizing a hummingbird has just buzzed past after it's already gone. He described carrying his friend's lifeless body up a mountain side from a helicopter crash in Afghanistan. He recounted the stertorous breaths of an enemy fighter he'd killed at close range dying in a language no one around him understood. (That soldier's copy of the *Qur'an* also had a place on Francis's shelf.) On a satellite call from Iraq he told me in a hollow voice that he'd accidently shot a translator attached to his unit during a firefight. I have no idea how many more incidents like these he kept to himself. The stories would fade rather than end.

According to his friend Matt, Francis was the squad's "designated marksman" in Afghanistan. Even though he hadn't attended the Army's rigorous sniper training, Matt said, soldiers who filled that role were sometimes called "squad snipers." Francis never mentioned this, or even that he'd earned a marksman pin, which I only discovered when I examined his medals sometime after we'd lost him. I have a photo of him with his rifle painted in camouflage, the Army's venerable M14, versions of which have been the standard weapon since the 1960s for killing a human target at a distance of nearly a mile, so far that the "target" never hears the shot that kills him, or maybe only its distant snap after he realizes he's been hit. I don't know how many nameless and distant fighters Francis also killed, but I do know he lived with their ghosts. And many others too – like the children whose bodies his unit collected after a bomb exploded near their schoolroom in Iraq. In shorts, a T-shirt, with a smart phone in his pocket, he was the Bush-era Man in the Gray Flannel Suit, one of the "invisible walking wounded," living with guilt and sorrow, dealing with chronic ailments, physical and mental, and bewildered at the disconnect between life at home and all he'd lived through overseas. It wasn't only he who was invisible, it was the wars themselves, for most Americans little more than gray clouds in the distance, blips on a TV screen that disappeared with a flick of the remote, links on the Web that were never clicked open, even as one decade of war passed unnoticed into another.

The Nootka Indians of the Pacific Northwest believe four generations of peace have to pass before a people who've gone to war will regain their sanity. If that required peace-time were compounded like interest for successive generations at war, America may be waiting a long time indeed for sanity to return. Wandering among the headstones, you can't help but notice that war or its shadow has been part of every generation. History's current runs from one war to the next here without straying down the countless byways of our cultural and social and political past. There's a fine simplicity in this version of history. Visiting here sometimes feels like carrying a tightrope walker's pole over a vast chasm, with the serenity and beauty of the setting at one end and the nature of the place – what it is and why it exists at all – at the other. Certainly it is a place to contemplate such notions.

Heather and I never imagined this part of losing our son, being here, that is, even in those moments when Francis was deployed and we feared the worst. How we might have imagined that seldom took us much past the moments when soldiers would appear at our door. We would know why they'd come as soon as we saw them. Returning from an errand to find a car parked in front of the house turned the last hundred yards up the street into a gauntlet of apprehension. Ditto a strange car turning around in the driveway or the doorbell ringing, with only a nine-year-old girl scout selling cookies on the porch. But nothing happens quite as you imagine it, or even close most of the time. Losing him in the way we did, years after he'd left the service, seemed – still seems – indescribably unfair.

The cemetery has entwined us in its history, past and future. A headstone from the Mexican War evokes the image of someone reading my son's name a century, two centuries from now. And while I may wish to think that visitor will find this place well tended – still under "perpetual care," as the VA's website confidently asserts – my friend Craig's ancient Indian tools are a reminder of how futile our best efforts are to immortalize ourselves. The people who made those tools once walked and lived on these very grounds. Who were they? What were their names? What kind of lives did they live? History swallows us all into obscurity sooner or later, and ultimately will swallow itself. This would be the place to insert a suitable quote on mortality from Ecclesiastes or a thousand other sources.

One of the most curious headstones in the cemetery reads simply:

TWELVE
UNKNOWN
INDIAN BODIES

The marker itself is undistinguished from others nearby. You can easily wander past it in the tessellation of thousands that surround it without noticing anything unique but for the epitaph – if your eye happens to catch it. In fact, I did just that a couple of times and finally made a special trip to view this grave after I learned about it, which, if you do visit, is Section 34, Row 21, Grave 8, across the lane from the old stone committal shelter.

These remains were unearthed over a century ago, when ground was broken for one of the buildings at the nearby Dwight D. Eisenhower VA Medical Center, originally known as the Western Branch of the National Home for Disabled Volunteer Soldiers and founded in 1886. The bones of these twelve bodies are collectively buried in a single grave in the oldest part of the cemetery. The surrounding graves are from the Spanish-American War. These people were probably among the few surviving members of the Munsee Tribe, which migrated to the Kansas Territory in the mid-nineteenth century. The street name of the cemetery's address, Muncie Road, is a token reminder of that tribe's presence here.

The Munsees, by then numbering fewer than a hundred, came here to rejoin the Lenni Lenape tribe, also known as the

Delaware Tribe, of which they were part. Their migration, as well as that of the Delaware, is but one fragment on a tragic and grand unwoven tapestry of discarded treaties and forced resettlements that stretches back into the seventeenth century and chronicles relations between European settlers and native tribes from the Middle Atlantic states, the Ohio River Valley, and finally what became known in the nineteenth century as the Kansas Territory. Curiously, even the name Delaware is not of native origin. The English named the river along which the Lenape once lived for the first governor of Virginia, Sir Thomas West, 3rd Baron De La Warr, and so named the tribe they associated with the Delaware River. According to Craig's 1857 map of the Leavenworth area, the cemetery and much of the surrounding land once belonged to the Delaware Indians, by then several times removed – in the active sense of the verb – by way of Ohio and Indiana and Wisconsin and Missouri from their native homeland in southern Pennsylvania. According to *The Encyclopedia of Native American Tribes,* the Delaware Tribe and its offshoots suffered more than forty removals from land granted by the U.S. government. By 1829 the tribe had been resettled in the Kansas Territory on a stretch of land that ran from the fork of the Kansas and Missouri Rivers at Kansas City northward through Leavenworth.

With the growing community that surrounded Fort Leavenworth, as well as the railroad under construction along the Missouri River, this land turned out to be valuable. The Delaware later ceded much of it back to the United States, reducing its tribal hegemony by 1860 to what came to be known, in the saddest, though surely most accurate, of geographic names, as the "Delaware Diminished Reserve." While these transactions made the Delaware one of the wealthiest tribes in the country, it's impossible to measure the financial benefit to one generation against the misery and cultural losses suffered by their ancestors over more than a century of removals and broken treaties.

Spread across 130 acres of rolling hills, Leavenworth National Cemetery overlooks a stretch of the Missouri River Valley, where the river separates Kansas from Missouri. From a hill on the east side of the cemetery you can look out over a wide expanse of land belonging to the Stigers Farm, so named for Stigers Island, which this section of land once was. According to Craig's map, a channel of water once surrounded it. The Army Corps of Engineers later redirected the river for the benefit of the railroad and the shipping channel, and so joined the island to the rest of the territory.

When heavy flooding inundated the upper Midwest in the spring of 2011, several months after we brought Francis here, the Army Corps released water from dams hundreds of miles to the north in Iowa and submerged the Union-Pacific railroad tracks alongside the river. The Stigers farm morphed into a vast lake, with muddy water rising so high the silos and utility poles in the distance nearly disappeared. Indeed, the tops of those structures were the only visible evidence this wasn't a natural body of water. So much for the Army Corps' efforts at "managing" the river, but that's a different story. It was a great comfort to us that the cemetery occupied high ground. From the crest of the same hill, you can turn around and look west for an inspiring view of the cemetery, with its wide fields and mature sycamore and oak trees and winding lanes. Straightaway on the opposite hill, mostly buffered by trees, is the complex of buildings that make up the Eisenhower VA Medical Center.

Whatever this land may become in a century or a millennium, it is maintained with great care now. The hallmarks of our national cemeteries are the uniformity of the headstones and precision of their alignment. If this cemetery were a poem, it would be a sonnet. The field's grade and contour create gentle sine waves in the sweep of the rows, which are aligned in startlingly precise rows and columns. The overall sight is hypnotic. As you drive slowly along the paved lanes and up and down the hillsides, they reshape themselves in kaleidoscopic Escher-like patterns. The uniform whiteness of the markers strongly affects these impressions. Quarried from underground mines in Mount Dorset, Vermont, premium marble is cut to the exact same dimensions for each stone: 42 inches in height, 13 inches wide, 4 inches thick. They all weigh 230 pounds. The stones are not embellished; they're all alike but for subtle design changes over the past century. There's something appealingly egalitarian in that sameness. It's not a little remarkable to realize that this meticulous design is fully at the mercy of Earth's whims, of heavy rains, long dry spells, the extremes of every season. So there's a subtext in the sight of these ranks and files too, in the fragility of their arrangement, despite the great care the cemetery receives, and the reality that it too will pass into the ages, like all that has previously passed on this land.

No matter the weather when we visit, I always open my window as we turn off Muncie Road and drive through the ashlar stone gates. The air feels different here, as if the place were drawing long, slow breaths and inviting us to share in its peace and serenity, and its past. I could be accused of several literary crimes here, from purple prose to the most pathetic of fallacies, but that sense of a place having its own breath is an image I owe to Francis, so its second-handedness is why my prose comes up short. It's from one of his phone calls home from Iraq and has stayed with me. It was characteristic of the quickness of his mind and sharpness of his perceptions. I had asked him what it was like to be there, in Iraq, what did the place feel like, and he thought for a moment, as if turning the question over (or maybe it was just the delay we always dealt with on his infrequent satellite calls). "You know how when you're in Colorado or somewhere out in nature," he said, "and when it's quiet, you can hear the Earth breathe? Well, there's none of that here. It's just dead. Everything is dead."

I suppose it's part of the weird, tilted logic of the universe Heather and I now inhabit that it makes perfect sense to me that a place for the dead should breathe with life, while for him, given why he was there and what he was doing, that place in Mesopotamia, the seat of Western civilization, should have seemed dead.

—∞—

It is evening. The maintenance crews have gone home. Lawnmowers and tractors cool in the dark tool shed and murmur in low metallic accents. Quiet reigns but for the occasional passing of a train or a jet overhead. Call it stillness rather. Quiet is such an elusive thing in our world, even here. A variety of birds thrive here – bluebirds, flycatchers, warblers, larks, jays. Hawks do profitable business from their perches in oak trees up on the hill. Kingbirds dart among the headstones, picking off insects, lighting on the branches of young maples that line the roadway. I trace the chiseled letters of my son's name with my fingertips in a numb kind of amazement that it should be here, those letters, engraved in marble and accumulating into the name we gave him almost thirty years ago.

Soon we have to leave. Fingers comb the grass over his ashes. I kiss the stone. We wipe tears, buckle seatbelts. Slowly ease down the lane.

On the way out a commotion in a stand of trees breaks the mood. We stop to see what it is before heading home.

Such is the place our son Francis rests.

This is one event that continues to unfold – not something that happened then, while this (whatever this is) is happening now. We are in the midst of a single event, and we don't even know how far along we are in its unfolding, or what we have yet to learn and experience.
—Journal, Jan. 10, 2013

Remedial Army

For death has made me wise and bitter and strong
And I am rich in all that I have lost.
—Siegfried Sassoon

WE HAVE ELEVEN HAND-WRITTEN letters from Francis during Basic Training at Fort Benning, more than he wrote in the next five years of active duty, including his deployments to Iraq and Afghanistan. We packed him off with a stack of pre-addressed, stamped envelopes and a pad of plain paper. We were so new to this we didn't know postage was free. All of his letters arrived on that stationery.

His first, dated May 28, 2002, twelve days after we'd seen him off at the airport, was particular about the format for writing to him. "Use black ink," he wrote, "and block lettering on the envelope and put the return address." Nothing in the envelope but a letter, photos, clippings, phone cards. And no packages. A week later, he added, "I thought I should tell you, also, make sure the envelopes are white. Someone got a yellow letter and they did 200 pushups before they could open it." He also thanked

Heather for a greeting card she'd sent. "The DS opens all the mail," he wrote, "and when a couple of guys started laughing, he told everyone to shut the f up because his mom sends him an f-ing card every week, and if they think it's funny, he'd give them something to laugh about." I could hear Francis grinning in his tag line: "It was cool." Years later we found that card among his things, folded, creased, as limp and worn as a garage rag from the miles it had traveled tucked in his pocket or helmet.

A letter endures, as William Merrill Decker notes, in a "continuous present tense."[1] So it is with the few we have from Francis, all written with a ballpoint pen on the lined notepaper we'd sent off with him. The pages have texture. They crackle and flutter. You hold them rather than scroll through a back-lit screen. Only one original exists, dated, signed, folded, slipped into an envelope, sealed on the tip of his tongue. The depression of the pen on the page, the curl of his handwriting – traces of him in motion, active, alive. Each letter a creation of hand and body, of language and spirit.

A continuous presence.

—⚏—

He was a good writer, if not a good student.

Graduated from high school, just. College not on the horizon. But with an IQ in the mid-140s, his aptitudes were high. I have a fixed memory of the sharp breath a school counselor drew when he reviewed Francis's first grade test results with us. He'd never

---

[1] *Epistolary Practices: Letter Writing in America before Telecommunications* (Chapel Hill: North Carolina U.P., 1998), p. 5.

seen verbal scores like this, he said. Nothing about his comment suggested hyperbole or flattery. He seemed genuinely wide-eyed. Francis had exceptional ability. He learned quickly, remembered things easily. He was both observant and witty, though his sarcasm could be acidic. We read to him from an early age, especially Heather. He loved books and reading and being read to. He spent much of a long car ride to Colorado when he was eleven or so buried in *D'Aulaires' Book of Greek Myths.* (We also had to backtrack twenty miles on that trip so he could return the trinkets he pocketed in a souvenir shop and offer a sullen apology to the owner as I stood by.) On a soggy camping trip years later, we were stuck in a tent for hours while heavy rain fell. He'd brought Raymond Carver's *What We Talk about When We Talk about Love,* a mature book for a seventeen-year-old, but also slender and light in a backpack. He read in fits while we were cramped inside the tent, not distracted when he put the book aside, but budgeting his reading, fearful he'd finish it before the rain stopped. Reading was a lifelong habit. One of my favorite deployment photos was taken in Afghanistan by his friend Jon Demler, a candid shot of a group of soldiers lounging in a shady, wooded area, helmets and armor off but weapons within reach. The others are talking or looking at digital devices, while in the foreground Francis is absorbed in a culinary magazine. His bookshelves at home were eclectic but rich – *How the Irish Saved Civilization, The Mutiny on the Bounty, The Invisible Man,* Colin Powell's *My American Journey, The Hobbit, Three Cups of Tea* (later, sadly, a discredited work), *China, Inc.,* Thomas Friedman's *The World Is Flat.* And two full shelves of cookbooks, nearly all of which Heather has kept.

But in school he was impatient, easily distracted, impish. We got regular calls and notes from teachers about behaviors, grades, problems. Conferences were always stressful. Years later, after he enlisted, I ran into his elementary school principal and we laughed about the time Francis got caught in fifth grade with a pocketful of condoms. How he got them, who knew? But at fifty-cents apiece there seemed to be a profitable market among ten-year-old boys with more ambition than prospects.

But he wro te well, and often more than well, with flashes of clarity and wit, in confident sentences and a clear and personable voice.

"Hi Everybody!" he greeted us. Or "Hello family!" Or "Hi Sommers!"

His new first name, we learned, was "You."

His letters are observant, descriptive. They tell stories:

> Then on Tuesday ... the gas chamber!! Everybody was really pumped to go through the CS chamber, but attitudes were different on the inside. I hated it. How terrible! At first with the gas mask on, I didn't think it was that bad, just a little burning on the neck and hands, and watery eyes. But with the mask off, I couldn't even open my eyes and all I could do was cough. Then someone dropped their weapon, so we got to do pushups. Like I said, I hated it.

The passage goes on to describe chemical warfare, the higher grade of gas they would face in battle, the Geneva Convention proscriptions against such weapons.

His letters have a sense of immediacy, high-end adventure, extreme scout camp, while Heather and I were mentally, and fearfully, translating these images into the realities of war. In the same letter, dated June 6, 2002, he shared this stark image: "On Monday we started training with our bayonets (which, according to the DS's, hopefully we will never have to use in combat). The bayonets are kind of a last resort, and that's why they are one of the first things to be taught." The open battlefield charges of past wars flashed through my head. Eye-to-eye combat. My son, a suburban kid who was on the high school wrestling team but never, that I know of, got into a real fight (and certainly not a deadly one), suddenly faced with this kind of terror. It was seeping over us at home, a slow leak, yet still distant. The U.S. presence in Afghanistan in June 2002 still had the trappings of a regional police action, while Iraq had not yet thrown the ominous shadow over us it would by that fall, nor did most foresee the bloody and long quagmire the invasion would unleash, or that an invasion was even certain. We were blithely focused on his spirits and even enthusiasm in boot camp, the ways he was climbing out of the sinkhole he'd stumbled into before enlisting.

A few days later, recruits are getting ready for their "first real road march with ... rucksacks (with 30 pound loads and bedrolls), equipment belts, weapons, and Kevlar helmets." He continues:

> I'm not sure how long it is, but I'm sure we'll be beat when we're done. By the end of training, we will have completed a 25-mile road march in all that equipment with the exception that there will be about 70-80 lbs. in our rucks (camping equipment, etc.). I have heard

> some guys in the church that are later in the cycle requesting personal prayers that they and their platoon will make it through that particular march.

The hard part isn't the weight of the pack: "… what's difficult is carrying your weapon at the 'ready' position. Especially in the early morning heat when the sweat combines with the moisture in the air and makes it really slippery." This was the kind detail that betrayed the quality of his mind. There was always a kind of offhandedness about dropping such images, written or spoken. He doesn't tell us it was hard, he shows us the hard. He never had ambition to write, but I always knew how good he might have been if he had. He created vivid images of Georgia in mid-June, when trainees at Fort Benning's Sand Hill found themselves clearing rattlesnakes from pits they dug to sleep in (or not), as the field buzzed and hummed and kept them vigilant all night, checking and re-checking boots and shaking out sleeping bags before slipping a foot into either.

He was meeting people from all over the country and, to his surprise, from around the world: "In my platoon there is a kid from Russia who's been here for 2 years. There's also a guy from the Caribbean and one from Mexico." And even more distant:

> At the Reception Battalion I was right in the mix with a lot of New Yorkers – mostly Puerto Ricans and from all five boroughs. I like listening to them talk – they have their own dialect going on. ("My dome looks mad crazy without no hair, yo." ☺)

He profiled the drill sergeants, too:

> The DS's for my platoon are probably about 26 and about 40. The older one is actually the cooler one. He motivates us a lot and likes to hang out in the barracks and answer our questions about Army life and tell stories. He served in Desert Storm with the 101st Airborne Division. The younger one is going to Ranger school this fall. All the DS's are either E6 or E7 – Staff Sergeant or Sergeant First Class.

Such details were not wasted on us. We were in Remedial Army, learning ranks, pay grades, what the different divisions did, where they were based, what a division was.

We are not a military family. Were not, I should say. No generational lineage of military careers on either side leading up to Francis's enlistment; no hearths filled with medals, photographs, or memorial flags looming when we visited grandparents, though both Heather's father and mine served in World War II, both in the Navy. Heather's dad deployed to the Pacific early on in the war, while my father's tour was something of a joke with him. He turned eighteen in midsummer 1945 and enlisted late in the war. Never sailed on a ship or left the continental United States. But the draft board still wanted him, so he joined the Navy rather than go into the Army. His favorite war story was about MPs appearing at his home to collect him only to find that he'd left for boot camp just days earlier. His tour lasted about nine months, during which he edited the newspaper at Camp Peary, Virginia, and played first base on the baseball team. My brother still has his glove, a floppy chocolate-brown pancake of worn leather about half the size of today's first base mitts.

Heather's father, Quimby, a few years older, had a more storied military career. The U.S. had not yet entered the war in Europe when he enrolled in journalism school at New York University, but he was eager to get into the war, so without telling his parents, he left school and hitchhiked to Canada, where he enlisted in the Royal Canadian Air Force. When the U.S. declared war several months later, Quimby was released and once more hit the road with his thumb out, destination San Diego, where he planned to enlist in the Navy. But he ran out of money in Amarillo, Texas, where a truck driver dropped him. With help from a couple of locals, he made his way to Dallas, where he was sworn in at a recruiting office. He deployed to the Pacific and served as a radio operator and gunner on a PBY-1 (the Navy's designation for a B-24) in Guadalcanal. He eventually became a radio instructor and was sent to Hutchinson, Kansas, where the Navy trained its airmen. There he met a seventeen-year-old girl named Mary working in a soda shop. Near the war's end, she left home and her cruel and hot-tempered elderly father and indifferent mother for good and traveled to Corpus Christi, Texas, where she married Quimby, who then soon put her on a train to his hometown, Poughkeepsie, New York, to live with his parents until he was discharged. They later had two children, Carol and Heather, and remained married for over sixty years.

When World War II ended, so did our families' brief military traditions. Like the fathers of millions of baby boomers, ours did their tours, took advantage of the G.I. Bill for college, and settled into suburban homes, pursuing careers and raising families. For Heather and me and many of our peers, the war descended behind a distant horizon that cast misshapen and faint shadows on the cave walls of movie screens and TV sets, which doubtless did more to distort our childhood understanding of war than enlighten us. TV shows about World War II in the early 1960s generally fell into one of two extreme categories: patriotic programs like *Combat, Twelve O'Clock High* (based on a movie), and *The Rat Patrol,* or slapstick comedies like *McHale's Navy* and *Hogan's Heroes.* The most wildly offensive program about war of that era had to be the comedy *F Troop.* Set during the Civil War, it brought inane images of war and ethnic stereotypes to a breathless low. A few lines from the show's theme song are sufficient to make the point:

> *Where Indian fights are colorful sights*
> *And nobody takes a lickin',*
> *Where pale face and redskin*
> *Both turn chicken.*

Our generation grew up exposed to a smorgasbord of dumbed-down, sanitized images of our fathers' war and war in general – American heroes versus sinister Asians, Germans, and Russians who spoke English in thick, disdainful accents. Blundering, evil, and uniformly poor shots, they always lost and Americans always triumphed. And history, from the American Revolution to World War II, as we learned in school, supported these jubilant endings. It's quite stunning to realize that the antiwar movement would germinate from within a generation raised on this medley of vapid programming. For the most part, our fathers allowed memories of the real war to slip away, or so it seemed. Like many veterans of that era, they rarely spoke of it. My dad had no lasting relationships with war buddies, no combat experience, no real sense that he'd even been in a war. Heather's father maintained a few long-distance friendships with veterans for decades through letters and holiday phone calls, but he shared little with his family about his tour in the Pacific, and although he'd been a Republican for most of his life, he abandoned the party over the Iraq War in later years and became a strident opponent of America's wars in the Middle East.

Heather and I are rooted in New York's Hudson Valley. The vast complexes of industrial militance – the shipyards and airfields and Army and Marine bases that dominate the economies and culture of regions they occupy – were alien places to us. As children, we sometimes witnessed the spellbinding sight of a National Guard convoy passing on highways between posts in Albany and Poughkeepsie. The Cold War was played out in air raid drills, vague calculations of our proximity to a Soviet nuclear missile's likely target in New York City or Washington, D.C., and the discomfiting cocktail of fear and envy when a classmate, usually with a smug pasting of schadenfreude on his face, described the bomb shelter his father was building. But the surreal prospect of annihilation was distinct from our childhood sense of real war – that is, war conducted on defined battlefields by men in uniforms that plainly identified them as good or evil – images that were shaped in the residue of our fathers' war and lessons in school about earlier wars.

Vietnam changed all that. For us, in college, the antiwar movement swept us into its current, while some of our non-college-bound high school friends were drafted after graduation. A few perished in Southeast Asia. The draft during Vietnam was done by lottery. My number, a lowly 69 (125 was the cutoff in 1971, my year), guaranteed that I'd be drafted if I didn't stay in school, and also quietly underscored one of the gross economic and racial inequities of that war. The draft created an army of mostly unwilling recruits who were physically unprepared and by many accounts inadequately trained. The all-volunteer force Francis entered over three decades later was a very different Army – populated by willing, often enthusiastic, recruits and spoken of with near-reverence in the media, in political discourse, and generally among citizens. He was joining the ranks of so-called "professional soldiers" and like many young men and women in the post-9/11 era, elevating his stature in the eyes of his countrymen, and more importantly to him and others, his friends and teachers and family back home. Enlistment sent a booster-shot of pride and confidence into a feedback loop that spiraled upward in the collective and singular purpose these recruits shared in the now-declared, newly-anointed Global War on Terrorism (GWOT – the acronym soon often written with creepy and knowing confidence by hawkish pundits without even reference to the term).

On a quiet Sunday at Fort Benning in early July, Francis wrote to us about a pro football player who would start training the next day:

Apparently he is (was) a safety for the Cardinals and turned down a big contract to train as an Airborne Ranger instead. I don't know the guy personally but if he's at reception right now, he may be regretting his decision a little. I think his biggest challenge will be keeping his cool around a bunch of guys who don't understand about discipline and doing the right thing and who weren't taking it seriously. I know I was surprised by some of the people here and how incompetent they are. As I write this afternoon, there are guys lying around sleeping when we were told all we had to do today after cleaning was stay awake.

So maybe not every recruit was stoked about the Army. A couple had gone AWOL, too, which the older DS shrugged off, saying he was surprised it took so long. Happened in every group, he added. More notable to us than a high-profile athlete showing up in camp was our son's remarks about "discipline and doing the right thing and … taking it seriously." We often read his letters aloud. This sentence earned a pause and wide-eyed exchange of looks.

Pat Tillman was the public face of waves of enlistees who rallied for months and even years in response to George W. Bush's "bullhorn moment" on the rubble of the World Trade Center three days after the 9/11 attacks. When a fireman in the crowd called to the President, "I can't hear you!" he responded, "I can hear you! I can hear you! The rest of the world hears you! And the people – and the people who knocked these buildings down will hear all of us soon!" To which the crowd cried, "U-S-A! U-S-A! U-S-A! U-S-A! U-S-A! U-S-A! U-S-A! U-S-A!" The fever of patriotism, the seductive narcotic of nationalism, the toxic desire for vengeance – all shaken and stirred into a septic cocktail whose cup Americans shared. On that same day, Congress passed the Authorization for Use of Military Force (AUMF), giving Bush a blank check for military action anywhere on the planet. A series of equally rash Congressional actions soon followed, including the Patriot Act and the Authorization for Use of Military Force Against Iraq Resolution of 2002.

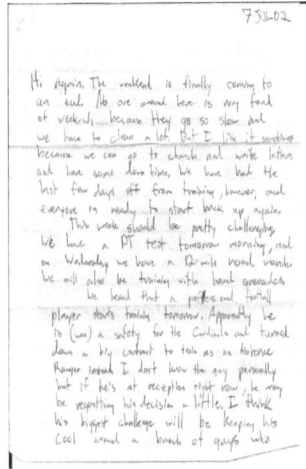

An intense atmosphere of tragedy – and victimhood – settled like thick fog over America, and we stumbled through it as well. Heather and I had experienced deeply the tragedy and sorrow of 9/11. In the days that followed, like many, we wept and called our families. But from beneath those events, worrisomely, a new lexicon began to seep into the language. America suddenly became The Homeland, an abstraction that was soon formalized into a new department and Cabinet position. The bloom of flags and bumper stickers everywhere – who was manufacturing all of these as the nation wept? – took on a threatening yet purposeful look. And we were more vulnerable than we knew.

The year or two leading up to Francis's enlistment had been a difficult time. Late one night when he was still in high school, a police car pulled up behind Francis and one of his friends after they'd just finished sharing a joint. They made a clumsy attempt to dump the bag of grass when they saw the cop, but too late. He had them. At home – the phone rang. Next, I'm sitting in a waiting room at the police station at 2:00 a.m. in jeans and a sweatshirt opposite another parent (who'd brought a lawyer), until they released Francis. My lawyer laughed when I called him. Should've let Francis cool out in a cell all night, he said. I did not share the joke. Like the condoms incident, it seems like small change now, but it consumed us then. And it was expensive. The drug possession charge landed us in court, followed by (fortunately) a diversion program and probation – and a long year for all of us.

After graduation he was amazed at how quickly the next year passed. He got a job in a hardware store and moved into an apartment with a crew that fed on low expectations and lurched from one dreary party to the next. He told me later how low he felt when a friend or teacher appeared at his cash register, about being seen there and having nothing but a shrug to offer when asked what his plans were (because if you're standing here at a hardware store cash register, of course you must have plans). He knew he was going under. America's entry into Afghanistan and the so-called War on Terror came at a moment when he needed a lifeline. The Army tossed him one – and us too, or so it felt. He came home one day with a stack of recruitment brochures and spread them out on the kitchen table. I was grateful he was willing to share this with me, with us, rather than simply showing up after it was a done deal.

Like many others, Francis was drawn to the glow of this moment. If Pat Tillman could give up millions of dollars, what did he have to lose after he finally lost even his job as a hardware store clerk for discounting some flowers for his mother? But that was a dead end anyway. On January 9, 2002, an Army recruiter, a staff sergeant, visited our home, impressively (and purposefully) dressed in his stiff, creased Class A uniform and speaking in the plain-speak of a not-quite-precisely-middle-Southern-maybe-sort-of-Oklahoma drawl, which we later discovered to be the ubiquitous accent of the Army, no matter a soldier's origins. At the kitchen table, after I tenuously suggested Francis take advantage of some of the skills-training he could get in really compelling work like heating and air conditioning or auto mechanics (yes, the Army has such training – or so the brochures said), he told the recruiter he wanted to do the hardest things you can do in the Army. I stifled a sigh. What the staff sergeant heard was enthusiasm, another kid who saw himself starring in a Rambo movie. A prospect who just wanted to know where to sign. I did too. But A) I never sign anything without reading it, and I wasn't about to let my kid do so, and B) I also heard echoes the recruiter could not hear – of personal expiation. Francis wanted to begin his life over again, to baptize himself, to wash away the guilt and regrets of a very young life already scarred by mistakes and transgressions in whatever the Army and this man in polished shoes and an olive green suit decorated in pallets of insignia and ornaments could offer him. The galvanizing effects of patriotism and the rush to vengeance and the magic of uniforms and the power of riflery and projected strength gave Francis and many others a sense of purpose. But for many, including Francis, Iraq would soon contaminate these illusions. Just two years later, a Marine in Iskandariyah, Iraq, where Francis was also deployed, told a *Washington Post* reporter why he'd enlisted: "To be honest, I just wanted to take revenge." And now he couldn't see any connection between 9/11 and the invasion of Iraq. "Sometimes I see no reason why we're here," he said.[2]

But in mid-summer 2002, 9/11 was a frequent topic among recruits at Sand Hill. "It was interesting to hear their different stories," Francis wrote, "about where they were and what they were doing on the morning of Sept. 11."

> The one I remember most vividly is this kid telling me how he ran all the way from where he worked in Manhattan across the Queensboro Bridge to Bushwick in Brooklyn, and when he got to his apartment the phones were not working so he had to wait all day for his family to come home to see if they were okay.

---

2 Steve Fainaru, "For Marines, a Frustrating Fight: Some in Iraq Question How and Why War Is Being Waged," *Washington Post*, Sunday, October 10, 2004, Sect. A, p. 1.

The mood of his letters is mostly upbeat. It's impossible to measure the gap between the reality of daily life in basic and the narrative he shared, but he was not given to hiding his moods. If things weren't going well, he wouldn't have written as often, if at all. And we'd have known it.

His first phone call from Fort Benning came two days after we put him on the plane. He was stressed, frantic even. The call left us more worried than reassured. It lasted about sixty seconds. A required call home: *I'm here, I'm alive, the plane didn't crash, I didn't run off!* I took the call and heard loud, harsh voices echoing all around him and finally a sergeant sharply telling him to wrap it up. Wasn't hard to picture the recruits lined up, waiting their turns for the phone, herded off to whatever was next – medical exams, shoe fittings, equipment checkout. In rookie military-parent time sixty seconds on the phone equals a week of worry and doubt. We parsed every syllable, every echo, every anything we could wring out of that call. Had he done the right thing? Would he make it through the next sixteen weeks? He said we wouldn't hear from him again for a while.

So his letters, which began to arrive the following week, were a welcome surprise and opened a window on a side of him we'd only glimpsed in recent times and a world about we which knew little. The writing was honest, we felt, and basic training maybe not as awful as we imagined after that first call. We knew he'd survive. There was enough bluntness, and snark, in his letters to authenticate them. But now, reading through them again, I also notice how often the word *fun* appears: "The past three days have been the most fun I've had since I've been here...." Then in the next letter, and without a hint of sarcasm, "This week should be fun." And later, ahead of a week-long camping exercise: "I think it will be fun, and even if it rains a lot, it'll be no sweat for me, right Dad? ☺" – referring to our soggy camping trip in the Rockies a year earlier. He also mentions that he hadn't seen any women since he arrived. Not surprising since infantry divisions are all-male and Sand Hill is segregated from the main base.

His sister Erin remarked that he only complained about one thing: complainers.

"Oh, well," he wrote, "imagine how it was 200 years ago."

That theme remained with him throughout his years in the Army, the perspective of history, how difficult life was for soldiers of earlier generations, how email, Skype, satellite phones, high-end running shoes and boots, and Gore-Tex had changed deployments. Years later he said boot camp was the easiest thing he ever did in the Army.

Basic was extreme summer camp for big boys. For most anyway, but not all. It was misery for those weren't in shape or were simply disillusioned and homesick and now realized too late that this was not for them. But Francis adapted and soon began to aspire to personal bests in physical fitness and getting to the top of his group. He was also writing about the newness of everything he was learning. The biggest thrills came when they began firing automatic weapons, tossing hand grenades, blowing things up, simulating fire fights in laser-tag exercises, paintball *in extremis*.

With all the confidence of a novice, and in chillingly detached prose, he instructs us in one letter on the proper technique for firing a rifle:

> The major trick is the trigger squeeze. If you squeeze to [*sic*] fast, your body naturally jerks in anticipation of the recoil. You have to go slow enough so that you don't know the exact moment of discharge....

None too comforting to parents, this new skill, his enthusiasm for firearms and detachment from their uses. In interviews with recruits at the Fort Benning website, gaming is the dominant metaphor for the firing ranges. Gaming on steroids. *Warcraft*-writ-large. *Assassin's Creed* ten-point-zero. Noise and action they couldn't dream up in their wildest, Red Bull-charged fantasies with a Play Station hitbox: three-dimensional imagery, monster woofers blowing back tidal waves of noise and heat from across an artillery range, the adrenaline rush of unleashing an M-249 Squad Automatic Weapon on a company of plywood bad guys. The Army's marketing wizards know their target market well, so to speak. Another dubious improvement over past generations of soldiering.

No blood, of course, in these video clips, no severed limbs, no hemorrhaging arteries, no shrieking in agony, no quivering with life-and-death fear, no torn, lifeless bodies, enemy or friend, civilian or soldier, woman or child. War is still an abstraction, draped in the haze of billowing flags and melancholy renderings of "God Bless America"; entwined in the indistinguishable urgings of patriotism and vengeance – and at Sand Hill, the excuse for big boys to play with expensive big-boy toys.

We were complicit. If we didn't share all of his enthusiasm, we were glad for his.

On our first visit to Fort Benning for Francis's mid-cycle pass, we stayed on post. We wanted to experience the Army up close. Heather and Erin and I went. Alex couldn't take time off from work.

There's a bitter and tragic irony in recalling our arrival. As we approached the front gate, we were confronted by the sight of a car so mangled into a clump of twisted metal and broken glass that at first glance it was unrecognizable for what it was. Where you'd expect to find a cannon or statue, instead this horrifying wreck was displayed on a blanket of manicured grass where no one coming or going through the gate would miss it. The message took a moment to resonate: a cautionary emblem against drunk driving. A message for *other* soldiers, we thought, not ours. It would be nine years before I'd visit a salvage yard in Kansas to claim a wreck just like this one, have the title transferred to my name, and arrange for the car's disposal just days after we buried Francis. But a great deal lay ahead before that day would come.

Not far from our rooms on post we strolled one evening on the quiet tree-lined lanes where officers and their families live in white clapboard homes and sedate duplexes with toys scattered on thin lawns now parched by the long hot weeks of summertime in Georgia. Several scenes from the movie *We Were Soldiers* were filmed here, including the powerful sequence in which the colonel's wife takes over the duties for a distraught mailman delivering casualty notices to the wives living on these streets while their husbands are deployed in Vietnam.

He wore a short-sleeve dress shirt, pressed olive-green slacks, and a cadet cap. Our photos reveal his misgivings about being seen in this outfit, which he wore for the first time that day, a requirement of the weekend pass. His belt buckle is askew and his shirt partly untucked in one picture. The confidence he'd enjoyed for weeks on Sand Hill in workout gear or utilities was now diluted by his first venture onto the main post in a blank uniform, devoid of color or rank – so obviously a trainee that he made an easy target even for a clerk in the commissary, who treated him with disdain and a clear sense of impunity about doing so as he got fitted for boots. (I was ready to give someone an earful, but he said I'd only do more harm than good, and I'm sure he was right.) Later in town, he failed to salute an officer, who sent a double-whammy his way but let it pass. Francis was so nervous walking past the man that he became flummoxed. The officer had the good sense to know this wasn't worth humiliating him in front of his family.

We toured the post, visited the museum, ate Chinese food. What he most craved was sleep, and he did – through Friday evening, while we went to a baseball game. Columbus, Georgia, is an Army town: fast food chains, tattoo shops, used car lots lined with rows of gleaming trucks and the promise of easy credit, quick-loan storefronts with barred windows. And a minor league team, the Red Stixx, Cleveland's single-A farm club. Minor-league baseball on a warm August night. Great seats for a nominal price and souvenir bobble-head dolls for each of us of the Goody-Goody Peanut Man, honored that night after thirty years of selling peanuts at this ballpark, which, sadly, was shuttered just a few years later. Heather's still stands in her classroom, an icon of good cheer to inspire her students.

Back at our room Francis slept on – right through until Saturday morning. We ate breakfast at the McDonald's on post, where he pointed out how many sergeants surrounded us. "The backbone of the Army," he said, echoing a phrase he'd picked up, proud of his own new standing. Rest and food had recharged him. The transformation was obvious, from his posture and fitness to his attitude. *Transformation* isn't quite right. These past twelve weeks had more accurately distilled him, exposing the essence beneath the encrusted layers of despair we'd seen before he joined. Here he was isolated from TV, from booze and drugs; physically challenged to extremes a high school coach couldn't demand without risking a lawsuit; fed well, but not overfed; made to take care of personal hygiene and belongings and living space in ways a mother could only dream of. Yes, indoctrinated too (though even that only served later to bring out his independent streak), but it was not possible then to say that this wasn't better than that; that the place he'd been before wasn't worse than the place he'd now landed. And no one felt this more than him.

The recruits were required to check-in at the barracks midway through the weekend. One minute late and the pass would be cancelled. We'd come over nine hundred miles for this visit and weren't about to have him swiped away. We made it with time to spare and then watched as several families saw their soldiers rush into formation just that late and then disappear into the barracks for the rest of the weekend. Another lost his privilege because he was out of uniform. Friends, girlfriends, parents all muttered in disgust at the injustice of it, but everything conspired to change the behaviors not only of these young men, but, it would seem, anyone close to them. To round out the weekend, recruits were drug-tested on Sunday night. Francis stood in line until 2:00 a.m. waiting his turn.

Mid-cycle is a misnomer. We returned four weeks later for graduation. This time we stayed in town. Enough full-frontal Army. Civilians are foreigners on an Army post. You need a military ID just to buy toothpaste.

Heather pinned his infantry cord on him at the "turning blue" ceremony the day before graduation. The platoon commander warned fathers, don't even think about trying to match pushups with your son. The ceremony the next morning was open-air theater staged on a wide tarmac field surrounded by dense woods. Outside the stands, hawkers sold flags and pins and tee-shirts.

A man wearing one of the black Army T-shirts recruiters hand out to prospects, sleeves torn off, hairy armpits exposed, an American flag ball cap pulled low on his brow, hurried his family along with a bouquet of small flags he'd just bought for them. As the band played, columns of soldiers made their way off-stage through the pine trees to the far end of the field. Soon the show began: marching drills, tactical demonstrations (we learned the components of a squadron that day – our education in All-Things-Army continued); a Bradley tank rumbling and spinning through its maneuvers; a thundering, smoky finale with blank mortar rounds exploding as "Bad to the Bone" boomed across the field. We cheered our soldiers like Ahab's crew on the quarter-deck of the *Pequod* as mortar fusillades shook the bleachers.

But it wasn't theater, this deadly business we'd taken up with these machines, this equipment, all this training, these young men in uniforms, the cheering and whooping crowd, who were no longer spectators but participants. More unsettling than the machinery and guns was their passion, which had given way to tribal instincts, and which were deeply seductive in this atmosphere, even for us. If others in the crowd, or on the field, had doubts, they were swallowed up in applause and smoke. I might have believed I was there to applaud my son's achievements – his personal victories, his renewal – but like Ishmael, my "shouts had gone up with the rest." The applause made no distinction between my intentions and the reality of the moment. Where I'd seen theater, others saw war and revenge – or equally as troubling, adventure.

The nation had not mobilized like this in decades. Here, it felt like all there was was war, and we'd been snatched into the gravitational pull of this black hole. Whether Francis had joined at the moment he did or later or not at all, this moment here, in this place, would have been played out, as it was many times again here and at bases around the country. A good friend, a Quaker and pacifist, expressed her disappointment with me when she learned that my son had joined the Army. Fort Benning, she reminded me, was the site of the School of the Americas (SOA). Yes, I knew that. I'd passed it, just a short walk from our accommodations on the first visit, a block from the commissary where Francis bought his boots. The SOA was the training center for U.S. interference in decades of elections and coups in Central and South America, including the 1976 overthrow of Argentinian President Isabel Perón and the atrocities that followed. My friend had recently traveled to Georgia to join in a protest against the SOA at the Fort Benning gates. Having a son here made me suspect. But years later, after years of war and after we lost Francis, she turned to me for advice: her son had just enlisted. He would train here too. How did I balance this contradiction, she asked, having a loved one – a son – fighting in a war that she (and I, too!) opposed? How do you maintain these two seemingly incompatible ideas? How do you live with them through the long years and terrible events that follow? It was not easy, often uncomfortable, and remains so, even now. But our sons and daughters make their own choices. Do we stop loving them when they don't choose as we wish? Do we fail to recognize their passions and commitments – as well as those of the people they will now depend on and who will count on them too?

Heather and I were more than uneasy about much of what we saw in the display of arms and bravado at the Fort Benning graduation that day. But we also met some of the men who trained Francis and would deploy with him. And we still, at that time (August 2002), did not know the U.S. would invade Iraq the following year and launch itself and the world into decades of conflict throughout the Middle East and beyond. Some on the field that day would not live through what came next. Towns and villages we didn't know existed and with names we couldn't pronounce or spell would be turned to rubble. Tens of thousands of civilians in foreign countries would die, uncounted and nameless to us. While our casualties would be listed each week in newspapers, scrolled across TV screens with billowing flags behind the passing names, those foreign deaths would remain clouded in numbers and buried in page six stories. *Fifty Iraqis killed over the weekend. U.S. airstrike at Taliban kills civilians, Afghans say.* So those Afghans say, so the newspaper says. Fear and confusion and bitterness had already choked our public discourse like the sulfurous smoke from these mortars. Years later, during a Memorial Day service at Leavenworth National Cemetery, where Francis rests, Heather and I bristled as a chaplain cheerily described how invigorating he found the smoke from an honorary cannon fusillade, the literal fog of war. That was the last service we attended there. More than a decade of war loomed beneath the horizon – and continues to this day – as we throbbed to *b-b-b-bad to the bone* on that overcast morning.

Heather: "Are you someplace safe?"
Francis: "I'm in Iraq, Mom. There is no place safe."

American Soldier

(Iraq, 2003-4)

I

"the face of America"

ARMORED VESTS. DESERT CAMMIE BDUs and K-pots. M4 assault rifles coolly slung from shoulders. Seriously badass game faces. Three soldiers stare at America from the glossy cover of *Time* magazine's 2003 Person of the Year issue. A woman in front, two men behind her, one white, one black. Three raveled in One, like the faith-bound mystery of the Roman Catholic Holy Trinity. A singular emblem of American might: The American Soldier.[1]

This winkingly inclusive palette has a subtext, and it's this: *Time* last recognized the American military in this way in 1950, when artist Ernest Hamlin Baker's watercolor rendering of a

---

1 "Person of the Year: The American Soldier," *Time* covers, Dec. 29, 2003. Web: http://content.time.com/time/covers/0,16641,20031229,00.html.

grim, unshaven, white, square-jawed Marlboro Man in a combat helmet was named Man of the Year, as he was then called. In the background, smoke drifts over the battle-wasted Korean countryside, where America wages its War on Communism. *Time*'s tribute to G.I. Joe: "Name: American. Occupation: Fighting Man."

The look had changed in half a century, but the language and tone had not. The write-ups for 1950 and 2003 differ only in geography and pronoun number. All that's needed is a bronze-voiced narrator to intone the melodramatic urgency of manly Cold War TV classics like *Superman* and *Dragnet*.

Here's G.I. Joe:

> He is more of an individualist than soldiers of other nations, and at the same time he is far more conscious of, and dependent on, teamwork. He fights as he lives, a part of a vast, complicated machine – but a thinking, deciding part, not an inert cog.[2]

A rickety paradox bounces through the passage like an old truck on a dirt road, but never mind. Imagine, rather, the military march that opened Walter Cronkite's weekly TV magazine, *The Twentieth-Century*.

[3]

Dahhh-dah-dah Dah-dah-dah-dah!

---

[2] "G.I. Joe, Man of the Year," *Time* covers, Jan. 1, 1951. Web: http://content.time.com/time/covers/0,16641,19510101,00.html.
[3] "The Twentieth Century," theme music composed by George Antheil. Web: https://www.youtube.com/watch?v=NuBZideXsK8. Notation transcribed by Dave Christi.

A parade into the American future on the cadence of American might.

And now, The American Soldier:

> They swept across Iraq and conquered it in 21 days. They stand guard on streets pot-holed with skepticism and rancor. They caught Saddam Hussein. They are the face of America, its might and good will, in a region unused to democracy.[4]

Trade a rickety paradox for a shaky pronoun reference (or Trinitarian mystery), but credit the nifty turn into the metaphoric "streets pot-holed with skepticism and rancor." We're only a breath away from George Reeves in leotards and a fluttering cape: ... *and who, disguised as Clark Kent, mild-mannered reporter for a great metropolitan newspaper, fights a never-ending battle for truth, justice, and ... well, you know.*

To treat *Time*'s selections as propaganda is the low-hanging fruit, though it still is fruit of the tree. But the editorial board is vigilant in qualifying its selections. Meghan McCain, who served on the panel that chose Mark Zuckerberg in 2010, voiced, in her own modest effort at Palin-speak, the meme that's trotted out annually to explain the magazine's sometimes disturbing ("Hitler," 1938), inexplicable ("Middle Americans," 1969), and just plain weird ("You," 2006) selections. "[T]he Person of the Year," writes McCain, "is an illusive [*sic*] title that has historically showcased, for better or worse,

---

4 "Person of the Year 2003," *Time*, Dec. 29, 2003. Web: http://content.time.com/time/specials/packages/0,28757,2006940,00.html.

the individual who has had the most distinctive impact on the previous year."[5]

Illusive or *elusive* – you could make a case for either.

Time's American Soldier issue appeared on newsstands days before Christmas 2003, and for all their mawkish prose, the editors were not wrong about that year's selection, nor would most Americans disagree with it. 2003 had most definitely been the year of The American Soldier, who, by year's end, had become the lodestone of American culture, and remained so for the decade that followed.

II
"Your [sic] *mine!"*

A weathered four-by-eight sheet of plywood leans on a fence post at the entrance to Squaw Creek National Wildlife Refuge, spray painted with the dates for hunters to invade the sanctuary and thin the deer population.

Warning or welcome?

If only deer could read.

It is a cold overcast Sunday in early January 2003, and our American Soldier still has a few days' leave before he rejoins his unit at Fort Drum.

Holidays over. Departure imminent. We've come here, Heather and Francis and I, to squeeze the last drops from his time at home.

---

[5] Meghan McCain, "Mark Zuckerberg, Time's Person of the Year," *The Daily Beast*, Dec. 16, 2010. Web:http://www.thedailybeast.com/articles/2010/12/16/mark-zuckerberg-times-person-of-the-year-defended-by-meghan-mccain.html.

"Come to the woods," exhorts Sierra Club founder John Muir, "for here is rest. There is no repose like that of the green deep woods."⁶

Not so deep or green today, Squaw Creek is a patch of wetland in northwestern Missouri, enclosed on all sides by human enterprise – industrial farms, a nearby town, and the interstate highway, which buttresses the eastern edge of the refuge. This is not our first visit. A decade earlier I chauffeured Francis and a minivan full of Cub Scouts here, careening north on I-29 behind a mom with another minivan full of scouts, who drove as if the gates of hell had opened behind her and my carload of squirmy, chattering ten-year-olds was the first squadron of liberated demons. The faster I drove to keep up, the faster she flew.

Canadian geese and other migrants frequent Squaw Creek on their journeys north and south, and so many geese gather here that the refuge also attracts the wildlife feature that brings most human visitors, like our Cub Scout troop that day – eagles. We'd, none of us, ever seen so many eagles – perched on tree limbs, gliding on thermals, pulling at the stringy tendons of geese ensnared in their talons, feathers hanging from beaks like smudgy remnants of finger food on the chins of ruminating children. We saw dozens and dozens of eagles that day, and their nests, too, some as deep as twelve feet, lifetime construction projects to which they return each year with life-long mates to nurture young and feed at this outdoor buffet, a Golden Corral of sorts for eagles. Still, whether resident or passing through, even then

---

6 Linnie Marsh Wolfe, 'John of the Mountains,' The John Muir Exhibit, Sierra Club website: http://vault.sierraclub.org/john_muir_exhibit/bibliographic_resources/book_jackets/john_of_the_mtns_wolfe_j.aspx.

these critters had become, as the phrase Wildlife Refuge suggests, refugees.

And now, ten years later, on the day of our visit, the geese are mostly gone, and a few eagles perched on barren limbs sadly eye the landscape like shareholders in a bankrupt company awaiting a miracle to redeem their worthless stock certificates. It's mid-winter but there's been little snow. A long-term drought has worked itself through the dry brown landscape. The water level in the marsh is low, exposing wide swaths of cracked bottom land where there had been marsh. But more than the season has affected this place. It feels like a microcosm of global imbalance; the drought an unnatural force, flocks decimated by jeopardies they face beyond the refuge – habitat loss, sprawl, herbicide-poisoned food sources, so forth, mankind in general.

Hot chocolate and sandwiches give us a lift. We stand at the edge of a quay and point to a few eagles here and there, both we and they looking over the desolate marsh like hungry diners who've just found the restaurant dark and its doors locked.

Francis offers little conversation. At this moment he has none of the fearsome confidence of *Time*'s American soldiers, though he is also, right now, the fittest he's ever been in his life. Training at Fort Drum during the fall, he said, had been much harder than boot camp. A tall, good-looking kid, at six-one and 180 pounds, he conceals his dark and thick blonde hair under a buzz cut. As a child he had platinum hair, which Heather allowed to grow into long wavy locks. Old ladies in the grocery store would preen over him – which he hated.

His moods are not new to us, but his darkness today has weight.

War is coming, and he is full of doubts about his decision to enlist a year ago, and fears about returning to Fort Drum itself, where he's been miserable since arriving there last September. His infantry unit in the Army's 10th Mountain Division had just lately returned from a year-long tour in the Balkans. Seasoned veterans with an FNG to pick on: a Fucking New Guy. Everyone on the post outranks him. Anyone can tell him what to do, and they often do. Pushups, latrine duty, hazing, which he refuses to tell me about, probably worried (with some justification) that I'll call his CO, or worse, write my congressman. He shares a room with a kid – *kid* = anyone ranked less than sergeant – he doesn't like. And Watertown, New York, not far from the Canadian border and bearing the brunt of arctic lake effect cold fronts that sweep across Lake Ontario, isn't known for its ambience. He does not want to return.

Impatience and frustration also swirl in a cocktail of loneliness and fear. In later years, Heather said she felt embarrassed for the world, the way you would for an unruly child at an upscale restaurant, or perhaps more apt, a drunken relative you'd brought to the company picnic. Francis, she knew, saw through its blunders and stupidity. And whatever else it may be, the Army is a sieve that catches more than its share of blunderers and idiots. All his platoon at Fort Drum had to do was square away the ruck sack packing list and they'd be done for the morning, but no, some kid shoveled clumps of dirty socks into his, so they unpacked and repacked and unpacked and repacked again and again and again. When another kid lost his night-vision goggles, worth thousands of dollars, the whole squad had to find them.

So it went. The tasks simple. The instructions plain – often stupid, but plain – in small words, easy to understand, but still some didn't, or thought it was a game, or were fucking around or hungover, or just didn't give a shit. All of the behaviors that led to low grades and discipline problems and troubles with the law before they got here were now seeping back to the surface like the stark, chill, relentless, it's-only-gonna-get-worse midnight dampness you feel rising through a cheap camping tarp thrown on wet ground as the rain pounds away on the tent. He was beginning to realize, Francis was, that the kids lined up beside him now might have to cover his ass when they were on their own in a hostile place surrounded by very determined men who preferred them to be dead and had the means and will to accomplish that end.

Over 60,000 American troops are moving into the Persian Gulf region as we sip hot cocoa and look for eagles at Squaw Creek. Another 100,000 by the end of January and 150,000 more in February. Meanwhile, the Brits announced a call-up of their own: they'll be deploying 1,200 troops. Cheerio! This is an American project, an American invasion and war, and it is without doubt coming soon, any day, following a long, intense build-up of arms and troops, and fear-mongering by the Administration and its apologists. By now, thanks to additional support for the war (and fear-mongering) in much of the corporate media, Americans have been mostly won over to the cause and along the way have become expert on a handful of factoids about the Middle East, which they recite to one another in coffee shops and kitchens and break rooms and garages and offices and warehouses and bars across the country. Cable-news reports on weather conditions; military strategies analyzed by talking-head-retired-generals-now-turned-analysts; names of religious sects and cities and provinces that few could have pronounced or found on a map only months ago – and many still cannot, even as they discuss and mispronounce them. "They hate our freedoms…"[7] becomes the national meme, as nationalism (but call it patriotism) morphs into jingoism. War is coming.

What do we tell a son who's plunging into this mess?

He's enlisted. He's committed. And now, so are we.

Well, there's this: he's not going to Iraq.

Even as the build-up along Iraq's border continues, his battalion is slated for Afghanistan. His utilities are dark-green camouflage. Afghanistan is what they trained for. Afghanistan is where Osama bin Laden and al Qaeda are hiding. He'll be hunting Osama. Iraq has nothing to do with Francis. He's going to Afghanistan.

There's pride in this. If also doubts. It's over a year since American forces entered Afghanistan. Francis likes to point out that 10th Mountain soldiers were the first regular Army boots on the ground in Afghanistan. There is still, we think (we believe, we want to believe), a just purpose in this war. In fact, it's not a war at all. Not an invasion. Not an occupation. It's a … what? A manhunt. A police action. Get the bastards and be done with it.

And it's not Iraq – and we question why we're invading Iraq and diverting money and forces to Iraq when Osama is in Afghanistan.

So we take cover from our fear and confusion in his pride. We squeeze out whatever good we can find in this for now, too.

---

7 "President Bush Addresses the Nation," *Washington Post*, Thurs., Sept. 20, 2001. Web: http://www.washingtonpost.com/wp-srv/nation/specials/attacked/transcripts/bushaddress_092001.html

During his leave, I asked Francis to wear his uniform for a few pictures. My own pride seems feels foolish now, and naïve. He didn't say no, but he made it plain that I'd just joined the ranks of blunderers and idiots as a charter member. Okay, so it was a hassle to put on the full get-up, and he could not, would not be seen or photographed without every buckle and button and shoelace in place. No halfway in wearing the uniform, almost as if he was more worried that one of the pictures would find its way back to his sergeant than too proud to dress halfway. And another thing – no smiling in uniform. Well, he was pissed at me – and the photos leave no doubt about that – but this was also a tic he'd picked up from the drill sergeants at Fort Benning, who wouldn't even crack a smile when we proud Moms and Dads snapped their pictures with our newly-blue-corded sons at graduation from Basic Training. He even, in keeping with the dress code, refused to wear his beret (his "cover") indoors or take it off outdoors – in our own home! He glares at me in the photos. We're walking the line – sloshing through bouts of pride – trying to boost his sense of same – and fear – he's volatile – he's had enough of the Army and wants not to be in it or put on the uniform or even hear about any of it while he's home on leave. It all sucks and here I am painting it in spangles and ribbons and bunting. Or so I must look – or so I am, because the reality of the moment makes it so. Family photos usually only show the smiles and joy, even if they last no longer than a shutter snap. So to have all of his moods, even the dark ones, is a way to keep all of him with us. I do, at least, have photos now from that moment in time.

But back to the point: dark-green camo, black boots, black beret, going to Afghanistan.

No doubt about that. Won't be deploying until late summer, but that's what they trained for and that's where they're headed.

Until they're not.

—⚔—

The random whoosh of a lone car out on four-lane, busy-all-day-long 119th Street. The *bip-bip-bweep-bweep!* of a police siren. The ear-scraping whine of a ninja-bike torqueing through redline gear shifts. Chasms of quiet in between. Here in our neighborhood it's dark and still. Good times for possum and raccoons, who amble across the street and raid compost bins with impunity, even arrogance.

O-dark-thirty on a week night. T-minus a few nights before he leaves. We're asleep upstairs, while Francis sits on the front steps smoking a cigarette (and maybe drinking a beer, though we don't hear about that later, so unconfirmed). Porch lights off. Concealed in the shadows of overgrown shrubbery.

Weird thing: it's January and warm enough to sit outside in a sweatshirt and smoke (and maybe drink beer). Next day, the temp will hit 70° F and I'll grill chicken on the deck. In January.

Right now it's dark and quiet and he's the only human on the street; the invisible drift of smoke, the amber tracer of his cigarette, the rustle of nocturnal critters the only movements.

Until, down at the end of the block, a car slithers out of the darkness, lights off, and cruises up the street like a snake gliding through still pond water. It slows to a stop a few doors down, pauses, and then rumbles to life, bouncing over the curb onto a neighbor's lawn and fishtailing through grass and flowers. Then across the driveway into the next yard and back into the street, where it idles for a moment like a runner sucking air after a sprint.

Francis flicks his smoke into the grass and wraps fingers around phone as the car cruises on, now passing our house and stopping next door. A new neighbor lives there. A single woman named Lou, alone in the house. Just moved here from Oklahoma. Forgot to shut her garage door. The car idles at the end of her driveway as if pondering its options, risks, prospects.

Car doors fly open and two men dash into the dark garage next door, one carrying a baseball bat. They're already through the inside door as Francis darts across the yard, shouting, erupting the still night, startling possums and raccoons, penetrating the sleep of sleepers on the block (though we don't hear a thing), which draws the intruders back outside, where they whip the bat around and dance past him, and then pile into their idling car and zoom off.

He calls the police but can't get a tag number in the dim light.

Lou doesn't even know these creeps were in her kitchen until Francis awakens her.

Right outside our bedroom window – Heather and I sleep through it all and hear about it in the morning. Lou stops by later in the day to thank Francis, and we sit on the deck and drink iced tea and get acquainted. In January.

Only time I was ever glad he smoked, which he soon gave up as he molted his civilian skin over the coming months.

Early that Saturday morning, January 11, 2003, we took him to the Amtrak station in Kansas City, where he would leave for Syracuse by way of Chicago. I'd reserved a bus ticket for the sixty-mile trip to Fort Drum when he arrived two days later. Union Station is a landmark in Kansas City. The intricately molded and painted ceiling of its Grand Hall rises nearly a hundred feet overhead. Massive windows with Roman arches throw light from the north and south sides of the building across the gleaming marble floors. During World War II, tens of thousands of soldiers passed through the Grand Hall. "Meet me under the clock" was the catch-phrase of that era. It's easy to fall under the spell of imagining the emotions shared here in those years.

A fitting place to see Francis off, or it once might have been. But Union Station was now a museum and closed at that hour on Saturday morning. A sign redirected us to a side entrance. We bypassed the Grand Hall and went down a dank hallway that smelled of stale food and diesel fumes and then opened directly into the biting, single-digit cold on the platform beside the idling train. We shuffled for warmth. Conversation was empty, utterances to fill the blank moments and mask the discomfort. It was too cold to remain here until the train pulled out. In my journal I described Francis as "shell-shocked." A cliché, an injustice to the horror of its real meaning from The Great War. I simply couldn't express the lingering image of his sadness at leaving, the hollow look of a child being sent off into the unknown, or worse, the well-known – now returning to the summer camp or boarding school where he'd only ever known torment. No matter the age, parents always see the child in their children. Later, Heather told me he said if he could have extended his leave by even an hour he would have. She'd fought off the urge to fall apart on the train platform. And his departure was harder for me than I thought it would be. This wasn't school or summer camp. The nation had sunk – was bailing itself – into two wars, and he'd soon be in the middle of one or the other (both, it turned out), and we all knew it. He was terrified – and so were we.

In the weeks that followed, these things happened: the space shuttle Columbia exploded on re-entry into Earth's atmosphere, instantly killing all seven astronauts on board, and then turning into a hailstorm of wreckage and human body parts that scattered for hundreds of miles across the Gulf states; Secretary of State Colin Powell addressed the United Nations to enlighten the world about the ominous discovery of aluminum tubes in Iraq – certifiable, gotcha-now, 110 percent proof that Saddam had weaponized poisons, though the world seemed to miss the observations of those engineers who studied Powell's speech and quietly reported that these tubes could not possibly be used in the ways he described; and at Fort Drum, a U.S. Army UH-60 Black Hawk helicopter on a training mission crashed in a wooded area. Eleven soldiers died.[8] This tragedy followed a similar one a month earlier in New Jersey, also involving a Black Hawk. The accumulating tension of these tragedies and imminent war gave us daily booster shots of anxiety before we'd even sloughed off the last dose. In his calls from Fort Drum, Francis was often gloomy and depressed. Tenth Mountain troops from another battalion would

---

8 "11 soldiers killed in Black Hawk crash," CNN.com, March 12, 2003. Web: http://www.cnn.com/2003/US/03/11/blackhawk.missing/.

soon deploy to the Persian Gulf region as the build-up continued, but he was still slated for Afghanistan, which oddly – in our then-simple-minded take on these conflicts – seemed (it is difficult to admit to our epic naïveté now) a better option at the time.

Heather and I visited Fort Drum in mid-March, with war possibly just hours away. We had good weather, which is rare in that season. Fort Drum, like most military installations, is an industrial complex. Touring it has all the charm of wandering around an electric utility plant. There's big, amazing stuff to gawk at – and take pictures of, which Francis fearfully said *Don't do that!* when I pointed my camera at a row of mortar cannons. I'd already gotten the shot. He looked around to see who might have noticed, but the street remained quiet and indifferent. Cannons and Humvees and tanks stood motionless. No sirens sounded. The forest did not suddenly awaken like Birnam Wood and come alive with MPs. But still, wandering around here with his civilian parents who were curious about everything he wanted not to think or talk about now seemed like a major hassle. The post is a cheerless place. And boring. And we were just trying to take in some of his world and make him feel good about it, whatever we might feel. Which was not good. He wanted not to be there as much as possible, so we took him to dinner in Sackets Harbor, a small nearby town on the St. Lawrence Seaway, which later gained fame for its upstart Kentucky Derby winner, Funny Cide. We also went to a movie at a run-down mall in Watertown. I don't recall the movie, but it did little to lift our spirits.

When war came on March 19, 2003, a few days after Heather and I got home, it felt – or the atmosphere that surrounded it felt – like the climax of a play in which we were now, in some bizarre

Pirandello-like way, both spectators and actors. There'd been all the basic elements of the drama: exposition (WMD reports and troop movements), foreshadowing ("The first sign of a 'smoking gun' ... may be a mushroom cloud."[9]), conflict (no explanation needed), intrigue ("yellowcake" / 9/11 attackers allegedly collude with Iraqi agents in Germany [never happened]). Rinse and repeat. Then came the spectacle: *Shock and Awe!* (Aristotle regarded spectacle as the lowest element of drama, though it now became the most captivating for Americans.) High definition fireworks, narrated by grim-faced anchors on millions of HD TVs for millions of spectators as thousands of Iraqi civilians were buried under Baghdad's smoking and crumbling buildings. America would be avenged for 9/11, Saddam taken down, Iraq conquered, oil revenue would pay for it all, and soldiers would, to a person in uniform, become heroes, as embedded reporters wearing clunky Kevlar vests and helmets that resembled Calphalon spaghetti pots told us from noisy and crowded trucks on the road to Baghdad. Their role in the drama to shore up the Administration's stewy message of patriotism, heroism, resolve, victory, freedom, Rambo on the move, John Wayne (who never served in the military in real life) taking that hill (or desert). "Surgical strikes," "targets of opportunity," "to disarm Iraq, to free its people, and to defend the world from grave danger"[10] – language itself warped to the purpose.

---

9 Jonathan Stein and Tim Dickinson, "Lie by Lie: A Timeline of How We Got Into Iraq," *Mother Jones*, Sept./Oct. 2006 issue. Web: http://www.motherjones.com/politics/2011/12/leadup-iraq-war-timeline.

10 Jesse Singal, Christine Lim and M.J. Stephey, "Seven Years in Iraq: An Iraq War Timeline," *Time*, Mar. 19, 2010. Web: http://content.time.com/time/specials/packages/article/0,28804,1967340_1967342,00.html.

Francis called that evening from Fort Drum to see if *we* were all right.

Although he was not supposed to go to Iraq – in fact, the war was predicted to end in just weeks or, at most, months – the sense that we had been launched into some terrible and cloudy future was inescapable. In just two weeks, over 8,000 bombs were dropped on Baghdad. We saw much of soldiers and embeds on TV, but little of Iraqis, unless they were waving American flags at convoys traveling north to the capitol, hoping, no doubt, the flags would inoculate them from attack or, for the children, bring showers of candy from the passing trucks. War in Iraq was all we thought about, but we knew we were not seeing the inside of it in these reports, and the atmosphere here seemed more celebratory than tragic. The stock market rallied some two hundred points when American forces entered Baghdad. March Madness was underway. It was a toss-up which mattered most. America would triumph, had triumphed, always triumphed. It would be over and done soon, though footage of unhampered looting and Marines toppling the statue of Saddam and hoisting an American flag, Iwo Jima-style, and reports of "insurgent" (a new word in the Iraq War lexicon, which we collectively adopted and put to use without wondering what it meant) forces seemed bothersome, even quietly troubling, though few thought these incidents mattered much or would last long, or so TV told us.

In mid-April, Francis called and said Afghanistan was still on the calendar for his battalion.

In mid-May, he turned in his green BDUs and was issued desert camo, but told us it was still Afghanistan.

In June, ditto: Afghanistan.

Also, he was coming home on leave, and oh yeah, he'd gotten a tattoo.

When he was in middle school, he said he wanted a tattoo. The season of inked-up skin was blooming. It was cool. Like Beatle boots when I was a kid, except you couldn't shove the ink into a Salvation Army box when the fad ran its course. Cool, I said, until you've had the same tattoo for thirty years, and your weight changes and skin dries, and … you know, you can't repaint your body like a house. You do know that, don't you? It's forever. At a stop light on one of those blistering hot summer afternoons when the air seems to dance like quivering Saran Wrap layered over the pavement, an old man driving a truck he might have bought used from the Joads pulled up beside us. The window was open and his dried-out, sun-burnt, shrunken biceps hung over the door. There in all its faded glory was a pale gray tattoo, design and lettering indecipherable, more of a smudge, like the markings on an old whale, than anything this dude might have once put there by choice. The man took a final pull on an unfiltered cigarette, flicked the butt off into the road, and spat heavily out the window.

"Wanna know what your ink'll look like in a few decades?" I said.

Francis smirked and shook his head. Wouldn't be him. Nope. Not never. He would always be young. What do old people know? Or parents.

A circular Celtic weave in a rich green and black on his right shoulder. He wanted us to know that he'd researched both the design and the artist before he had it done, and I have to admit, it was beautiful and unique – and striking, too, that he wanted to celebrate his Irish. He laughed at guys who went in for the mystique of Chinese characters they could neither read nor pronounce – and which might say anything. And better yet, those who now lived with bad grammar and spelling etched into their bodies: *Your mine! Nothing last's forever.* Maybe not, but for sure a lifetime.

The first hint we had that he wasn't going to Afghanistan came in late July. All he could tell us was that that deployment was now in doubt. A few weeks later, in August, we learned that he was heading to Iraq. A rumor went around among the soldiers that a master sergeant in the battalion had a jones for Iraq, where all the action seemed to be, and didn't want to miss out before he retired. That's what Francis told us. More likely, as Matt McKenzie later shared in an email – inserting an "LOL!" – that rumor just gave guys in the outfit a scapegoat when they learned their orders had been changed. No chance, Matt said, that a battalion master sergeant would have that kind of pull. Rather what happened was this: The 10th Mountain's 1-87th Infantry Regiment had deployed to Afghanistan in 2001 as part of Operation Anaconda, following the 9/11 attacks. McKenzie was with the 1-87th then and later reassigned to Francis's company in the 1-32nd Infantry Regiment. Since the 1-87th already had experience in Afghanistan, they would redeploy there in 2003, while the 1-32nd would become the first 10th Mountain battalion sent to Iraq.[11]

11 Matt McKenzie email, May 5, 2016.

Losing Francis

Francis departed on September 4, 2003, flying out of Fort Drum on a C-17 headed for Germany and then Kuwait, the staging area from which the battalion would proceed north into Iraq. He called home late that afternoon before he boarded the plane. An unusually long call. As always, he couldn't say anything about the itinerary. It was an awkward call. He wanted to stay on the line but didn't offer much conversation and couldn't talk about WHERE HE WAS GOING! So I filled the minutes with chatter about stuff that would really interest him, like the chores I was doing when the phone rang, his sister Erin's next choral concert at school, and that ever-reliable phone-convo-filler: the weather. Heather soon arrived home and took the phone. Then Erin turned up and got on too. Then me again. But he did not want to hang up as long as he had time on his card. And he was getting more worked up the longer he stayed on. We were just plain running out of stuff to talk about. Doubtless, too, our anxiety vibe pulsed through the phone as we grappled with how to give him closure so he could leave us behind and do whatever he needed to do. He was facing a year in Iraq. The only reasons it might be less were unthinkable.

We heard from him again late that night, now calling from Germany, where he had a four-hour layover. Two days later, he called from Kuwait, about noontime here (8:00 p.m. or so there). The call was disjointed, full of static, with a lag between speaking and hearing that created an echo effect and became a pestilent feature of every call for the next year. He was posted at Camp Udairi, whose construction *Stars and Stripe*s had lately celebrated in a feature article. *Camp Udairi: Massive U.S. military compound rises in Kuwaiti desert,* the headline lauded. A phoenix risen from the sand. The write-up only wanted music by John Williams: "Convoys of bulldozers and graders stir up huge clouds of sand on a future runway while soldiers hoist new tents, working furiously to build this new Army airfield before the beginning of war."[12] So much stirring and hoisting and furiously working and building newness for the newest new beginning of a new war. Words to moisten patriotic eyes, spark shivers in the spines of the Yankee Doodle Dandiest among us.

Closer to the Iraq border than our suburban home is to downtown Kansas City, Camp Udairi was part of a patchwork of camps throughout northwestern Kuwait. Francis said the wind was unrelenting, blowing sand into everything – food, nostrils, lungs, underwear, socks. The temp was over 100° F twenty-four-seven with no relief. His tone had not improved since Fort Drum. He also said that once they started moving north we might not hear from him for as much as two months. And as always, he couldn't tell us where he was going.

These phone calls have no precedent in military history. During World War I, British soldiers fighting in trenches along the frontline in France were so close to home that they might be on the battlefield in the morning and back in England on leave in time for tea that evening. Still, news traveled slowly then, and more often was suppressed for propaganda purposes. Poet Wilfred Owen, a lieutenant in the British Army, died in battle five days before Armistice Day, November 11, 1918, but his parents did not learn of his death until five days later, while all around them

---

12 Steve Liewer, "Camp Udairi: Massive U.S. military compound rises in Kuwaiti desert," *Stars and Stripes*, February 15, 2003. Web: http://www.stripes.com/news/camp-udairi-massive-u-s-military-compound-rises-in-kuwaiti-desert-1.2056.

the nation celebrated. An enduring emblem of family separation in wartime, Homer's Odysseus is gone from Ithaca and his wife Penelope for twenty years, ten alone to return home from Troy, and she has no word of him all that while, as she weaves and unweaves the fabric on her loom to put off her suitors. Fictional, mythical, yes, but also emblematic of what war has meant to families from ancient times to the near present: separation, distance, not-knowing. But now our son was talking to us in real time from a war zone on the other side of the world. We had this fragile connection through a microwave signal that stretched invisibly from the phone at his ear to a satellite orbiting in the exosphere and then back to a cell tower on earth and into our fiber optic landline in Kansas and invisibly across the room to our cordless phone. It is a notion that easily ignites one of those random epiphanies of wonder that bubble up about driving an automobile, flying 500 m.p.h. at 30,000 feet, or flipping an electric light switch on after mankind – and all of life on the planet, for that matter – has known only sunlight or firelight or darkness until the most recent seconds on Earth's geological clock. We had no personal experience of separation by war with which to compare it, but this still felt strange, unnatural, inconsistent with inherited, even innate, notions of war. And what would it mean on a vast social scale that war could be fought in ways that now wove Skype and email and Twitter and satellite phones into the fabric of war itself? This perceived nearness? For soldiers and loved ones, this straddling of worlds and erasure of distance and time?

For one thing, the near end of letter-writing. His handwritten letters from basic training in Fort Benning were doubtless accountable, in part at least, to both the cloistered nature of BT and orders from drill sergeants. We had none from Fort Drum and only a few while he was deployed. I'd also given him a blank journal before he departed, thinking he shouldn't pass up the chance to document his experiences (maybe more my instinct than his), but to my knowledge he never jotted a word and I never saw the journal again.

When he left for basic, I resolved to write him weekly. Long, discursive, wordy, often banal letters, recounting sports, yard work, weather, bird sightings, concerts, house painting, more weather, deck painting, outings, movies watched, books read, family visits, still more weather, snow shoveled, leaves raked; queries about how he's doing from neighbors, friends, family, and coworkers; also banking, taxes, questions about what he needed, what his friends needed; questions about whatever he could tell me about whatever the fuck they were doing over there, and weather. I often wrote in a journal format, making regular, dated entries throughout the week, so he sometimes got near-daily, possibly numbing, accounts of our life here. They went on for long, dense, single-spaced paragraphs and pages, one every week. I look at them now and wonder why I lingered over some of the trivia I shared and cringe at tortured passages of over-written prose. But I wanted to fill the pages with home, with chatter, with enough detail to keep him preoccupied for an hour, to send letters he couldn't read in one sitting but rather would pick up again when he had down time. Mail, Francis's squad leader, Spc. Paul Zundel, later wrote to us in an actual letter thanking us for some packages sent to the squad, is the "best morale booster that we have here in Iraq."[13] In keeping with that sentiment, I skated over politics, which in some ways made little difference since he was already there, and the politics that got him there as *fait accompli* for us as it was for him. Besides, I didn't so much believe anything I might write about politics would undercut him in whatever ways he was adapting to what he had to do, but rather that he'd agree, even sympathize with me. He already had enough doubts of his own, and doubt is not a helpful sentiment in a war zone. Whether that was the right choice is easier to judge now, but then, he was there and we were here, and our job – my job – was to help him survive.

So the phone calls also had the unintended consequence of keeping him, at first, and others throughout their tours, from fully landing where they were. They distracted many soldiers. By his second tour, in Afghanistan, Francis openly complained to us (in emails) about guys dealing with marital and girlfriend problems, childcare, car repairs, house repairs, and always finances on satellite calls from outposts in the mountains. Distractions, he complained, that might get people killed.

We had one more call from Kuwait, on September 12, 2003, 4:30 a.m. our time. He'd been left behind by the convoy, he said, and would be traveling into Iraq "by other means," which he couldn't say. Turned out his company flew. If anything happened to him, he told us, we'd hear from the Army before it was on the news. Comforting. My journal entry for that date also notes that President Bush reassured Americans that the chances of getting injured or killed were greater if you lived in California than in Iraq. However one interprets that bit of solace, there is

---

13 Letter from Spc. Paul Zundel, undated, circa Feb. 24, 2004.

no positive construction for it. By now it was obvious that the Administration's plans for an easy victory in Iraq had crumbled. Two weeks later, Francis called from Iraq. A "shithole," he said. They were living in warehouses and had no hot meals. He'd been so rattled in these first weeks that he forgot his weapon one night when he was roused for guard duty.

His battalion was there to establish Forward Operating Base Chosin at the Musayyib power plant, near the town of Iskandariyah, where he would be posted on-and-off for much of this deployment. McKenzie later told me that at some point in this deployment they were in every major front in Iraq – more than we learned from Francis, who often kept things from Heather and me. Each day brought news of 2,3,4 soldiers killed in Fallujah or Karbala or Mosul or around Baghdad. Casualties mounted. Dozens of names in the paper each week. Two men from Francis's unit were killed in early October[14] – the first he'd known personally, and the first memorial service he attended, which he described as "very tough."

It was getting very real. By mid-October 336 troops had died in Iraq – 216 since Bush's May 1, 2003, announcement of the end of "major combat operations" in Iraq.[15] Francis did not forget his weapon again.

As we passed through October and into a cool and rainy November, our lives were loosely hinged to everyday activities we'd have been doing whether or not Francis was in Iraq, but

---

14 Spec. Steven L. McGowan, "Chosin Battalion soldiers honor fallen brothers," *Fort Drum Blizzard On-Line*, October 16, 2003. Print copy. Web version no longer available.
15 "U.S. Commander killed in Iraq firefight," CNN.com, Oct. 17, 2003. Web: http://www.truth-out.org/archive/item/45931-us-commander-killed-in-iraq-firefight

now there was a remoteness to all of it, as if we were watching ourselves play scenes in silhouette behind a backlit scrim. Alex had his own apartment and stopped by one evening with a box of homemade cookies, an unusually domestic gesture for him. Erin was a senior in high school. She ran on the cross-country team, and Heather and I were active in the booster club. I edited the newsletter and photographed the races, a great distraction for me that fall. We attended every meet and had the team to our house on a couple of Friday evenings during the season for pre-race-day pasta feeds. Spaghetti for thirty. A tornado of kids and parents blowing through and then off to the football game – and per coach's orders, not one kid failed to find us and say "Thanks for the food!" ("No problem.") That month, too, Erin and some 400 kids at school came down with a vicious strain of flu. All of these happenings were the membrane of life that concealed a burning core of worry and doubt and anger, like the thin layer of atmosphere that gives life to the earth while a molten stew of rock and minerals blazes away deep within the planet's heart.

Heather tumbled through bouts of worry about Francis that bordered on depression. She was up past 2:00 a.m. one Sunday night writing a letter and packing a box for him. Usually we'd do these packages together, but I found this one taped shut and addressed the next morning. Fifteen soldiers died that day when a Chinook helicopter taking them on leave went down. The flood of casualties played on our nerves. The next day we attended Erin's cross-country banquet. She confessed to Heather that she missed Francis so much that she wrote him a letter *during* one of her final exams. We were bouncing like ping-pong balls over the net between the world that surrounded us and global events that writhed their way like tentacles into our lives, between our anger at the war and our worry for our son.

On a call in late December, Francis told Heather that his squad was going out on a mission and we wouldn't hear from him for at least a week. He sounded as anxious, Heather said, as when he first landed in Kuwait. Erin got on that call too. Later, when we decorated the Christmas tree – our first with him gone and just three of us to trim the tree because Alex was working – she wanted to hang his favorite ornaments. Moments of recognition. The wars were spilling over onto our whole family. News of casualties, battles, and the political chaos that surrounded the Iraq war poured into our lives through an open spigot, particularly that December as American troops engaged the first battle of Fallujah, some of the fiercest all-out fighting since the invasion. On Christmas Day 2003, we heard from Francis, now back from his mission. To Fallujah.

III

" ... everybody knows the enemy only uses chemicals on Wednesdays."
—*Francis*

He called again on the second day of the New Year. His friend's nose had been blown off by an IED. The attacks continued, as did the missions – often at night, at high speeds, which Francis later described as terrifying. The squads would travel with lights off because they were easy targets on isolated, pot-holed, unlit roads. IEDs might be anywhere.

Still, maybe not every moment was full of dread. Francis's squad leader, SSG Chris Bryant, told me years later that then-Specialist Sommer was the only driver he'd ever seen pull a Hummer up on two wheels in a hard turn, which he'd done for the thrill of it and no other reason. Bryant was awarded two silver stars for bravery in Afghanistan, but not before Francis scared the shit out of him in Iraq.

After hearing about the IED attack, Heather was distraught for the rest of the day, distant, quiet, and what little she said always found its way back to that incident. It wasn't just that that might have been Francis, but that someone had been injured, someone to whom we now had a connection, and that he was someone's son or brother or husband. Francis was hard-wiring us into the war itself and all of its horrors.

News from Iraq offered no relief. A week after that call, a Black Hawk helicopter was shot down in Fallujah, killing eight soldiers.[16] A few days later, two soldiers died in an IED attack there.[17] Three weeks into the new year brought the total of U.S. soldiers killed in Iraq since the invasion to over 500. The intensity of the fighting and frequency of casualties were unrelenting. I began capturing these reports in files, in some vague way believing I was archiving the war before each incident was lost in the chaos of whatever followed, or more likely, so it felt, simply swallowed up in the white noise of NFL playoffs and NCAA basketball. Former Army officer Andrew J. Bacevich, at once a self-described conser-

---

16 "Black Hawk crash kills 8 in Iraq," CNN, Thursday, January 8, 2004.
17 "Iraq Roadside Blast Kills 2 U.S. Troops," Associated Press, January 24, 2004.

vative and harsh critic of both the war and President Bush, also took note of this seeming incongruity: "In the midst of a global war of ostensibly earthshaking importance, Americans demonstrated a greater affinity for their hometown sports heroes than for the soldiers defending the distant precincts of the American imperium."[18] Perhaps not so incongruous if waging war depended less on the support of American citizens than their indifference to it.

Three years later, in May 2007, when Francis had just returned from Afghanistan and was only months away from leaving the Army for good, Bacevich lost his son, First Lt. Andrew J. Bacevich, Jr., in a suicide bombing in Iraq at age twenty-seven, the same age as Francis when he died in 2011. Just weeks later, Bacevich wrote an opinion piece for the *Washington Post* in response to a couple of emails he'd received blaming him for his son's death, "insisting," he wrote, "that my public opposition to the war had provided aid and comfort to the enemy ... that my son's death came as a direct result of my antiwar writings."[19] Having lived through the loss of a child, I find it difficult to imagine the kinds of bottom-feeders who would write such things to a newly-grieving parent. But ignorance is a pre-requisite for a want of empathy, and theirs includes a failure to understand this basic notion: that asking "How am I to blame?" is a condition of parental grief. Bacevich didn't need prompting to search his own soul for complicity in his son's death, but his response must have

---

18 Andrew J. Bacevich, *The Limits of Power: The End of American Exceptionalism* (New York: Metropolitan Books, 2008), p. 131.
19 Bacevich, "I Lost My Son to a War I Oppose. We Were Both Doing Our Duty," *Washington Post,* Sunday, May 27, 2007. Web: http://www.washingtonpost.com/wp-dyn/content/article/2007/05/25/AR2007052502032.html

disappointed the bottom-feeders, if they bothered to read it.

How do you oppose a war while you have a son fighting in it? I understood the quandary Bacevich faced. I shared it. And the question is not new. Whether one is an antiwar activist or quietly and privately opposes the war a loved one has been sent off to fight, some families have faced this dilemma in every war. One of the most outspoken opponents of the British entry into the first world war was the fiery suffragist leader Charlotte Despard, whose brother, Sir John French, commanded the British Expeditionary Force. Yet throughout the horrors and carnage of that war, arguably worsened by her brother's poor decisions in his command role, Despard maintained a close and loving relationship with him, writing in 1917, at the depths of the war, "He is, I think, dearer to me than anyone else."[20] Like the Iraq War, The Great War of 1914-18 was not only pointless but tragically consequential, as it planted the seeds of the major global conflicts that followed throughout the century. Unlike Iraq, during which less than one percent of the American population served in the military, World War I touched nearly every family in England. Whether conscript or volunteer, every eligible man either served, most in France and Belgium, where over two million died, or had to account for why he didn't. These included the sons and husbands and brothers of thousands of antiwar activists who faced the dilemma of hoping for the safe return of loved ones while opposing the war itself. Many lived with the personal conflict of knowing that as wrong-headed, and even criminal, the decisions were that led to that war, and still more

---

20 Quoted in Adam Hochschild, *To End All Wars: A Story of Loyalty and Rebellion: 1914-1918* (Boston: Houghton Mifflin, 2011), p. 284.

so to its perpetuation, they also wished for success in whatever form it might take, for failure could only be worse.

Bacevich's opposition to the Iraq War began, in a sense, long before the war itself. The 9/11 attacks, he wrote, had led him "to promote a critical understanding of U.S. foreign policy." But America was in no mood for critical understanding, and with little opposition, Bush got nearly unlimited authority to invade Iraq on the premise that it was a "preventative war" – a war, Bacevich believed, that was unwinnable. His response, as he describes it, was through his writings and speeches to join his voice with "teachers, writers, activists and ordinary folks – to educate the public about the folly of the course on which the nation has embarked.... I genuinely believed that if the people spoke, our leaders in Washington would listen and respond. This, I can now see, was an illusion."

For promoters of the Iraq War, Bacevich was an uncomfortable opponent. A graduate of the U.S. Military Academy at West Point, and later professor there; a Vietnam veteran; a retired Army colonel, he doesn't remotely fit the stereotype of antiwar activists. He's no middle-aged hippie or ex-Weather Underground dissident. His books and essays offer a clear-headed view of American exceptionalism and empire-building in the Middle East and across the globe for the enrichment ExxonMobil and Texaco and Conoco and the imposition of neo-liberalism glazed in the shimmer of democratic values. In response to the bottom-feeders, he wrote, "As my son was doing his utmost to be a good soldier, I strove to be a good citizen." Opposition to the war, in this sense, was a conservative value, and the radicals were those in the Administration who were flouting the Constitution and Geneva Conventions, as well as the United Nations, in pursuit of this war, whose purpose seemed to shift with the political winds.

My own center of gravity in the personal dilemma of opposing the war while Francis was deployed was strengthened by getting to know others in the antiwar community. The late Kris Cheatum, for instance, was a leader in PeaceWorks Kansas City, which has its roots in the anti-nuclear movement of the 1980s. Kris was a seventy-odd-year-old-woman, who, along with her late husband Lynn, was for years a fixture at antiwar demonstrations every Sunday afternoon at Kansas City's Mill Creek Park. On one Sunday, I saw a man who towered over this diminutive firecracker berating her about how we should all be supporting the troops. In a firm but disarmingly agreeable voice, she responded, "I can't think of a better way to support the troops than by bringing them home!" It's a moment that stayed with me – both what she said and how she said it.

As it was for Bacevich and the Cheatums, protesting the wars was also for me an act of citizenship. Which in the eyes of a few still left me suspect on both sides of the question, though I found Bush supporters who wanted me to tell Francis "Thank him for his service" more discomfiting by magnitudes than the handful of war opponents for whom my anti-warism litmus paper was faintly tinted because I had a son in the Army. I met several people who either openly or with a doubtful glance expressed just that sentiment. One was a grieving parent, so what could I say? Another, a woman who declared, "I hate war!" as if to suggest that my son must love it. Why else would he become a soldier? She had her passion and he had his. First World Logic. Maybe I should have asked if they continued paying taxes while we were at war. The wisdom of the incisive, and belated, retort, or the better part of discretion. But I never asked. More than a third of our tax dollars – some $650 billion a year – support this military adventurism. An estimated $4.79 trillion have been sunk into Iraq and Afghanistan as of this writing.[21] So are those people who are willing to rebuke my son for becoming a soldier in an unjust war also willing to pay the crushing fines and possibly do prison time to support their belief that we should not be at war? Their annual (or quarterly, for the more affluent) payments to the IRS also render them complicit in supporting the American military enterprise. Shouldn't they withhold one-third of their taxes, the amount that pays for these wars? How different is risking a fine or prison time for not sending money to Washington every year from facing a certain court martial and prison term at Fort Leavenworth for refusing to fight? In fact, very. Who has more at stake, a delinquent taxpayer on American soil or a soldier who lays down his rifle in a war zone, where the penalty is a near-guarantee of prison time and a possible death sentence? The question of complicity isn't so clear for some, like me, while cognitive dissonance is a fog many are stumbling through, only they don't know they're in a fog. For me the premise was false simply because the blame for these wars doesn't lie with the soldiers who fight them. They're just an easy target, so to speak, for some ... thankfully, only a few.

---

21 Neta C. Crawford, "U.S. Budgetary Costs of Wars through 2016: $4.79 Trillion and Counting," Watson Institute of International Affairs, Brown University, Sept. 2016.

Losing Francis

The heaviest costs of these wars have been borne by the people of Iraq and Afghanistan. My journal entries for 2004 are a near-daily catalogue of casualties, which include many more civilians than American soldiers. In mid-February, over 150 Iraqi civilians, most of them men who'd lined up for jobs with the Iraqi Army or police force, were killed or injured in near-simultaneous car bombings in Baghdad and Iskandariyah.[22] Reuters reported that 20 people were killed when a car bomb ripped through the police station in Iskandariyah.[23] But that incident, we learned, was much worse than that.

Francis mentioned it in an email to Heather, sharing little of what he'd seen firsthand:

> Don't know if there was anything on the news about the recent car bombings in my sector. No soldiers were hurt, but about forty civilians were killed and the surrounding city blocks were an absolute nightmare. We'd never seen anything like it. The next day people were coming to the FOB asking if we knew anything about missing family members of theirs. I can't wait to come home! I'll call soon.
> Love,
> Francis[24]

---

22 Edward Wong, "The Struggle for Iraq: Combat; Up to 80 Killed In Bomb Blasts At 2 Iraqi Sites," *New York Times*, Feb. 11, 2004. Web: http://www.nytimes.com/2004/02/11/world/the-struggle-for-iraq-combat-up-to-80-killed-in-bomb-blasts-at-2-iraqi-sites.html?_r=0
23 "Car Bomb Kills at Least 20 South of Baghdad," Reuters, Feb. 10, 2004.

The bomb also destroyed a school across the street from the police station. Children were among the casualties. Francis's unit was sent there to collect the bodies. Years later I asked Matt McKenzie what happened. In a lengthy email, he said the police station had been targeted because insurgents regarded them as collaborators. The bomb, he added, was "huge":

> There was a school across the street and at least 55 people were killed with well over 150 critical injuries. We were called to cordon off and help clean it up. When we started to walk around, you couldn't help but step on body parts and flesh left everywhere. It was by far the most horrible thing I have ever seen, and I'm sure it was that way for Francis. They were picking up body parts and throwing them into huge plastic garbage bags, and then would throw the bags in the back of pickups. Sometimes the people would just toss the bags and they would hit the side of the truck, bust open, and body parts and blood would scatter all over the side of the truck and back on the ground. There were dead women and children along with the men. There were more innocents killed than the actual target of the police station. And again, it was one of those things we talked about after the incident, couldn't believe it ... and that was it, it was over.[25]

Over?

These stark images stayed with Francis, who years later described the scene to me in similar detail, including the nauseating sensation of his boots slipping on human flesh and organs splattered on the ground.

---

24 Francis Sommer, email to Heather Sommer, Feb. 12, 2004,
25 Matthew McKenzie, email, Dec. 17, 2015.

Word came in February that the 1-32 Infantry's tour in Iraq would be extended, end-date unknown – which meant a stop-loss for anyone in the unit who was on short time for discharge from the Army, including Francis's roommate, who by now had become a close friend. Francis wasn't caught in the stop-loss this time; that wouldn't happen to him until Afghanistan. But anyone who was caught affected everyone in the unit. The extensions and this policy made the politics of the war personal. In a March 2004 email to his uncle, Chris Sommer, Francis wrote plainly about the pressure on soldiers nearing the end of their active duty tours to re-enlist:

> Hey uncle! I have been following some of the political news you wrote about and I think my vote will be going the direction of someone other than Bush. It really sucks for a lot of the guys around here that were getting out and now they're stuck over here. The worst part is how the higher chain of command is pushing hard for them to reenlist. I don't know how people stay in the infantry for twenty years ....

We didn't hear from him again for weeks, until one Sunday morning in late March. Heather and Erin were at church. I had just heard a news report about rocket attacks in Baghdad, including ten explosions in the Green Zone, when he called.

He was shaken. His vehicle had been the target of an IED that day, the closest he'd come yet. His Humvee was one of hundreds of vehicles convoying the Marines who would replace the 82nd Airborne at Iskandariyah. Francis's vehicle was targeted because of its light armor. His team was given the day off. Not for the first or last time, he asked me not to tell Heather what happened.

One of the men injured in that attack was his friend Shane, whom we'd met at the Kansas City airport when he and Francis left for Basic Training at Fort Benning. The two were formed into a "unit" by the recruiting sergeant, with Francis in charge – his first leadership role in the Army (and a crumb to inflate the innocent pride of his parents) – because he was a couple of months older than Shane, which meant he'd carry their documents. Heather and I saw Shane again at graduation from Basic, where we met his mother, too. Francis and Shane had remained together throughout training and were later assigned to the same company and squad at Fort Drum.

The explosion ripped through the side of the vehicle, knocking Shane unconscious as shrapnel slashed into his back, torso, legs, and kidneys. He was treated in Iraq and then flown to Landstuhl Airforce Base in Germany for further treatment, and finally sent on to Walter Reed Hospital in Washington to recover. Another soldier lost his hand in that attack.

A month or so later, we learned that Shane had returned home to Independence, Missouri, and we invited him to come visit us. He sat stiffly in an armchair and shifted about frequently, saying he had constant back pain and still had shrapnel embedded in his body, which he'd have to live with for the rest of his life. He was cheerful in a visiting-the-parents-of-my-soldier-buddy kind of way and said more than once that he'd rather be back in Iraq with his squad than here at home. Not an uncommon mantra in an era when squads remain together throughout training and deployments, unlike Vietnam, when draftees were pulled out of their units in the field and replaced as soon as their two-year tours ended, creating squads that were less cohesive. The visit was warm but awkward. Shane assumed the role of booster, telling us how brave Francis had been in the fighting, but his cheeriness also glazed over details, as if he were varnishing whatever they'd experienced for our benefit. To him, we were Frank's parents: we needed good news, to hear how courageous our son was, how loyal and steady and competent. So that's what he shared. The visit was uncomfortable for Shane in more ways than back pain; it wasn't the kind of thing he'd ever done before or, I think, wanted to do again anytime soon.

By early April 2004, battles raged in more than a half-dozen cities in Iraq, including the 2nd Battle of Fallujah, which in its first week saw 12 Marines and more than 30 Iraqis killed, women and children among them. Francis emailed his Aunt Nancy (my sister) describing how hot weather only led to more fighting: "It's funny how violence picks up with the heat around here, and we've had to be more active now that winter is over. I am quietly hoping we'll be gone before it gets too hot, not only to avoid the danger but because when you live in a tent there's nowhere cool to go in 130 degree weather."[26]

On April 18th I received this email from Francis – addressed to me only:

> We will be moving up north to a camp near Ramadi and Fallujah in the next couple days. We have been extremely busy and for the last few days we have been in a defensive position around a bridge on the main supply route that was expected to be blown

---

26 Francis Sommer, email to Nancy Allen, Feb. 27, 2004.

up by the enemy. Because of all the activity security was at a maximum and we are recovering from having slept about 4 hours in the last four days, plus a mortar attack on our perimeter. I am a little anxious about the move and frustrated because we have gotten to know this sector, but word is the new camp has better facilities (chow hall, etc.). I will send any new addresses if we get one for the new camp.

Here's one not to tell Mom: HUGE firefight the other night. The biggest since we've been here. I had my hand on the side of a cargo Humvee and I could feel rounds ricocheting and blowing past my hand. The CO was thrilled about it (he's sick like that), and we took no casualties. Not a scratch. Yesterday the LT pulled a round out of his shoulder pad. We all grumbled about the shoulder pads, but hey, the shit works!

The biggest impact it had on me was how close they were; right off the road. I don't know whether to take satisfaction in this, but I do: I had eyes on someone shooting from behind a rock and I fired at him and when I stopped to look, he was all crumpled up and falling on the ground. Maybe I should've taken leave. Tell Mom I love her.

Love, Francis

Should have taken leave because he was nearly killed or because he killed an Iraqi fighter – or from realizing that he'd found satisfaction in doing so? He'd also, I began to notice in his emails and calls, become more open and frequent in expressing his love, as if he wanted to be certain it was the last thing he said to us if we did not hear from him again.

He hadn't mentioned killing anyone before now, though it's clear even in these few sentences that this wasn't a first. In fact, Shane had described his tenacity firing the M2 .50 caliber machine gun from a turret on the back of a Hummer during a firefight. "You should have seen him firing away!" Shane exclaimed when he visited us, thinking how proud we'd be. The chaos of fragmented images that crowded our heads at that moment needs Joycean prose to render. We could only nod stiffly.

The "sick" CO Francis mentioned was his new Marine commander. His battalion had been treated well under the Army's 82nd Airborne, he said, but all of that went to hell when the Marines arrived and hung their banner on FOB Chosin. He emailed us a new address and a few observations about life with Marines in charge, shared here verbatim (arrows, parentheses, exclamation mark, sarcasm, and all – except the zip code):

> From: Frank Sommer
> Sent: Wednesday, March 31, 2004 6:05 AM
> To: Heather Sommer; Robert Sommer
> Subject: New address
>
> New APO (thanks a lot Marines):
>
> SPC Sommer, F
> C CO 1/32 INF
> 10th MTN DIV
> Camp Iskandariyah ← optional!
> APO AE [xxxxx] ← note the change

Yup, the Marines are making their impression felt around here, to say the least. I thought the Army had some stupid rules. Here's a couple:

—Protective masks will be carried on your person every Wednesday. Because everybody knows the enemy only uses chemicals on Wednesdays.

—Every convoy to leave the wire will have a minimum of 7 vehicles. We've been using 3 or 4 for small missions. That's twice the number of people that will be brought into harm's way for something as simple as escorting the water truck around town. It's also pretty hard to tactically insert troops into a nighttime observation point with 7 hummers hogging down a dirt road.

—Manned battle stations with drills taking place weekly. In case Haji starts swimming across the Euphrates to take over a camp of 800 armed personnel and heavy artillery.

Oh, well. 5 months left. Talk to you later.
Love, Francis

He soon returned to Fallujah, where his unit was tasked with defending a firebase just outside of the city. The fighting there was so intense that when we heard from him again, the unit had briefly returned to their FOB for fresh clothing and ammo *because they'd nearly run out!* He described an AC-130 gunship destroying several buildings. On TV we saw images from Fallujah of Iraqi dead in the streets, including children. After that we had no word from him for several weeks.

On May 10, 2004, the phone rang at 4:00 a.m. He'd been

relocated to a new FOB, Camp Manhattan, an Army base near Habbaniyah Air Field, about 50 miles west of Baghdad and halfway between Ramadi to the west and Fallujah to the east. The heat was ferocious, *averaging* 115° F or more. We could hear fatigue in his voice. His unit had been on continuous missions, sleeping only one hour in twenty-four for days at a time. I'd recently purchased a National Geographic map of Iraq and now began to understand the military focus on this area. There's an oil field in Fallujah, while Camp Manhattan is adjacent to Lake Habbaniyah on the south and the Euphrates River to the north, a location that has had strategic value since the British occupied the area during World War II. All of these towns, including Abu Ghraib, are on an 80-mile stretch of Highway 11, which bisects Iraq and runs from Baghdad all the way to Syria.

We rarely talked politics on calls with Francis, but that morning he brought up the atrocities at the Abu Ghraib prison, which were all over the news in those weeks. His disillusion with the war was beginning to surface, and he resented how these events reflected on him and other soldiers. "Support the troops, not the war!" he said sharply, abruptly. The first time I'd heard anything like that from him. A week later a civilian captive in Iraq was beheaded by extremists in retaliation for Abu Ghraib. Here at home, Senate hearings on the matter were a clusterfuck of stonewalling, white-washing, and finger-pointing. The commanding general of the prison not only walked away without consequences, but even landed gigs on the speaking circuit, while the only two people sent to prison were a sergeant and a private.

During that month, I was reading Stanley Karnow's *Vietnam:*

A History. The parallels between that war and Iraq were streaming like centipedes off the pages and onto my skin, leaving me bristling as I read. It was all there – the propaganda, the escalation, the civilian casualties, the hidden enemy, the other-ness of the people whose country we occupied, the abyss into which we were falling with no bottom in sight. 2004 was an election year, and now, as was also true during Vietnam, every wartime decision seemed to be before all else a political decision. By April more than 700 American lives had been lost, with some 3,000 injured. In just over a year since the invasion, over $200 billion had been flushed into Iraq with no end in sight.

IV

"There's an old saying in Tennessee – I know, it's in Texas – probably in Tennessee – that says, fool me once, shame on – shame on you. Fool me – you can't get fooled again."
—George W. Bush, Sept. 17, 2002[27]

Erin graduated from high school in May 2004, an honors student, hard-working, active in school, hanging out with good kids (except for a mean girl or two). Heather and I threw ourselves into "Project Graduation," an all-night lock-in party at a local bowling alley. Arrowhead Stadium during a rare playoff game would have seemed like a refuge for meditation and yoga

---

27 Jacob Weisberg, "W.'s Greatest Hits: The top 25 Bushisms of all time," *Slate*, Jan. 12, 2009. Web: http://www.slate.com/articles/news_and_politics/bushisms/2009/01/ws_greatest_hits.html

compared to the chaos of that long night. Still, for a moment life seemed good, so much so that Heather said "it would be completely perfect, if only Francis were home." We got home at dawn, scooped out a couple of bowls of ice cream, and then, before collapsing into bed, turned on CNN, where we learned that another soldier had been killed in an IED attack in Fallujah.

We didn't hear from him again for several weeks. He called sometime after midnight on June 5th and described a recent mission. His platoon had been sent out to "pick a fight" with insurgents in a village near Ramadi. They surrounded the village during the night and blasted Arabic recordings at sleepless residents, bating insurgents to come out and fight. Then they poured heavy metal rock music into the village while squads went house-to-house in search of weapons and enemy fighters. But they found nothing and no one wanted to fight, and in keeping with his lifelong streak of bad timing, Francis's platoon, he learned later, missed out on a barbeque at their camp while they were out in the desert entertaining Iraqi families with heavy metal all through the night, as they kicked in doorways and tore their homes apart.

The horrors continued. Several hostages were beheaded that month and next. In late June, we saw video footage of a Korean man pleading for his life moments before he was murdered. A week later a Marine of Lebanese descent died in the same unthinkable manner. Fighting raged throughout the country, with American deaths now cresting 900 and injuries over 5,000. On Independence Day, we were so sickened by all of it that we skipped the fireworks and went to the movies – to see Michael

Moore's *Fahrenheit 9/11*. It seemed an especially patriotic thing to do. Our nation needed rescuing not from Iraqi "terrorists," but from the extremists at home who were peddling fear and had delivered us into this war as a means to save the withering presidency of George W. Bush. The movie is not only an incisive critique of the inept and corrupt leadership in the White House – and its connections to the bin Laden family – but a peeling back of all the layers of fear and misrepresentation that had led to the war and now promoted it. I was so fed up after seeing the film that late that night I wrote an email to thank Michael Moore for making it. "This administration is the worst in the history of this country," I wrote at the top of my lungs, "and we are sick of being manipulated and lied to."[28] My email later found its way into a collection of similar notes from service men and women and their families, entitled *Will They Ever Trust Us Again?* – "They" being soldiers who were sent into this war based on lies and fabrications. Heather felt the same outrage and added her name to the email as co-signer when the book was published. My anger – our anger – seemed only matched by the intensity of the war itself. We sat nightly over dinner working ourselves up as we recounted the falsehoods and propaganda we heard from Administration officials each day. Erin has a phrase for conversations like ours: "violent agreements." That was us, violently agreeing on all that was wrong with this war. Bush had broken faith with the single greatest trust a president possesses – and it was being abused in the most craven manner imaginable.

---

28 Michael Moore, *Will They Ever Trust Us Again: Letters from the War Zone* (New York: Simon & Schuster, 2004), p. 189.

This breaking of faith had filtered its way throughout the Republican Party, as neocons and evangelicals gained ground with each election. As war raged that summer, the Senate obsessed about an issue of even greater national security than our foreign wars: gay marriage. Then-Senator (and later – sadly for us in Kansas – Governor) Sam Brownback produced charts that weirdly, bizarrely, somehow "concluded" that gay marriage led to an increase in out-of-wedlock births. The logic of this was …? We were tumbling through a nightmare of lunacy – we'd fallen into the rabbit hole. Language itself seemed to have no meaning because there were no longer logic, facts, truths, even words, as W reminded the world each time he opened his mouth. Anyone could say anything and it had the same merit as anything else. Opinion was fact, and facts were whatever you believed to be facts. War raged but Senate Republicans only cared about gays. The election loomed; the hate wing of their party needed red meat and Americans at large needed to be distracted from war.

I threw myself into the election that summer, making calls, walking neighborhoods, helping local candidates, desperate to see Bush & Co. sent packing, if not indicted. Heather was consumed with worry about Francis, often spending hours checking news from the Fort Drum and other websites. She bought a subscription to the *Watertown Daily Times* on-line. We heard from Francis again midway through July, now back at Iskandariyah. Ten months in hell had seasoned him. He described a convoy of replacement troops from the 10th Mountain's 2nd Brigade arriving in Humvees with no doors and gunners standing in the turrets, "stuff," he said, "our unit would never do." The heat was averaging 115-20° F. Tents were too hot to be inside during the day, which meant getting no sleep if you'd been on duty all night. Equipment malfunctioned in the heat, too, and soldiers were being served, at most, one meal a day and some days none at all. Heather thought he sounded mature. I did too, but the call left me really pissed off.

Then came a 2:00 a.m. call on Saturday, July 25th. Even after months of random calls like this, the phone shocked us out of sleep. Heather awoke in panic, afraid we'd miss the call or hit the wrong button and drop the line – or that it might be the call we most feared. He was okay, he wanted us to know. Not reassuring when that's the first thing he says. FOB Chosin had been hit. A mortar barrage had destroyed the entire camp. He was hasty and direct, and the connection was terrible. Two men from the 10th Mountain had been killed. The battalion was moving up to Camp Manhattan again, and the soldiers, he said, "had nothing left but the clothes on their backs." He couldn't say more about it. Heather got on the line and grew more and more agitated as she knelt over a pad on the floor and shook the pen to make it write. Afterwards she stayed up for the rest of the night searching the Web, sending e-mails, getting a box started to send to him.

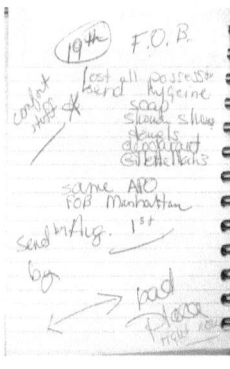

Losing Francis

Mortar attacks on this FOB were frequent. This much we already knew. The chow tent was hit in one attack. Fortunately the only casualty from that incident was that troops had to eat MREs until it was rebuilt. Francis had given his brother Alex a lighter picture of these attacks in an email earlier in the year:

> They've been keeping us pretty busy lately, and we've kind of been on our toes 24 hours a day after some recent rocket attacks. It was actually kind of comical in a sick way the other night after we heard an explosion in the camp at about 2 am, then a few seconds later you could hear everyone's sleeping bags unzip and people knocking things over in the dark trying to get out to the shelters. Oh how I love this place.[29]

Iraqi fighters would set up on the far side of the Euphrates River and lob rockets into the base. Francis said they were lousy shots, so as dangerous as the mortars were, they seldom hit anything and the enemy could pack up and disappear before a rapid-response team mounted up and drove to the nearest crossing. Putting in on the river would have left teams loaded down with body armor and equipment vulnerable to attack and drowning. But on this day insurgents poured over forty rockets into the camp, destroying most of it and killing four soldiers. Photos later released by the Army showed row upon row of smoking, twisted metal-frame cots; mattresses disintegrated; tents gone. The rockets had found the ammunition bunker, setting off a blaze that consumed everything.

29 Francis Sommer, email to Alex Sommer, March 1, 2004.

An attack this devastating must have been all over the news, Francis thought. It had happened five days ago. He was certain we'd be sick with worry. Now he was finally able to call so we'd know he was alive.

But we hadn't missed news of the attack. It wasn't reported. Nothing. Nada. A couple of lines about casualties from a generic bombing somewhere in the vastness of Iraq. This was the first we heard of it, and now in his voice we heard something else too – betrayal. How could we not know? Men died, a post destroyed, troops on the move because there was nothing left of their camp – and no one at home knew?! Recognition, disbelief. His voice dimmed. Words … came … slowly. The reality of our ignorance seemed to spread through his consciousness like a noxious transfusion flooding his veins, and then it infected us, too. Indeed, how could this be so? Whatever we thought of this war – whatever anyone thought – we were at war. The nation was supposed to be at war – so the leaders told us – but how vast was the geography of all we did not know about this war, how much lay beyond the horizon?

Heather attended church that Sunday morning. A friend named Anet asked about Francis. It whelmed up. Heather told her about the call, the bombing, the casualties, the "nothing left but …," so forth. With no thought it would go farther than that. Unloading. Emotions frothing.

But Anet, a Mary Kay sales pro … not so reticent. She told the pastor, who quietly tapped an email to his flock, which then, within days, raised $1,000 for supplies for Francis's squad. And more: energetic and determined Anet led

Heather on several shopping expeditions for hygiene items, running shoes, food, skin lotions(?) (she was with Mary Kay, and those boys were in the desert sun, so okay, skin lotions), which were then packaged and sent to the company chaplain in Iraq.

Meanwhile, at home that same Sunday morning, I opened the *Kansas City Star* and read a letter by a fellow citizen who'd grown tired of reading about all the unpleasant news from Iraq.

"Good Iraq news!" the letter-writer proclaimed.

A "positive article" had finally appeared describing America's great achievements in Iraq. Such reports were "long overdue," she declared. "The United States has done a wonderful job of improving lives in Baghdad, getting power grids running, schools back in session, businesses open again. Life is better than before."

Huh???!!!

... better ... than ... before ... ?!

July 2004 had been one of the worst months yet in Iraq. While the toll of American lives lost since the invasion now exceeded 900, the best estimate of Iraqi dead was over 13,000.

But for this letter writer such news was just more evidence of the liberal media bias that suppressed all the "positive" news from Iraq.

Umbrage. Outrage. Open laptop. Type with fists.

A week later my response stood where my fellow citizen's had, the same column, the same font, a couple of paragraphs. An angry yawp. A whimper. Prufrock objects. It felt hollow to see it there. Nothing changed. Nothing ever would. So it felt.

Francis's battalion was living under the cloud of a possible extension that summer. He'd written in June that there was "a strong likelihood … that we will be extended for up to six months beyond our initial twelve." His own frustration with the war and its conduct were now undisguised. "I don't think," he urged me, "a quick note to a state representative would be overstepping any bounds." We caught a similar drift in an email Francis's squad leader, Spc. Paul Zundel, sent to Heather's church in gratitude for the care-package effort, though for his audience's sake (and any officers who might see the note) cheerier and more discreet:

> Me and the rest of the guys in my squad are truly grateful for the care packages your church has sent to us. Mail is the best morale booster that we have here in Iraq. We are also happy to have you and people like you back home who think, pray, and appreciate our efforts. Sometimes you catch yourself in a daze, wondering what and why do we have to be here in a land that does not take kindly to the West. The kids over here sum it up when you see them. The girls are the ones who get me the most, because of the way that their culture is and the lack of respect and rights of the women here. Really the hardest part of the job here is not knowing. Since our battalion is attached to another division, we are being kicked around between the Army, the Marines, and our division who wants us back for Afghanistan in '05. We don't know if we get leave or if we do, when it will be. We don't know when we are coming home, we're guessing September.

So even if the end of the tour came on schedule, the battalion was already facing redeployment to Afghanistan the following year.

In August, we went on short-time, counting the days until Francis's company returned to Fort Drum. But the fighting only seemed to intensify, as a siege began in Najaf, where insurgents took refuge in a mosque, more or less daring Americans to level the building and create a site of martyrdom for Muslim pilgrims for a thousand years to come. All that was clear about this war was that it was chaos, mingling religious and sectarian conflicts with the political agendas of thousands of corrupt regional officials and misguided foreign agencies. It was simply a mess – and without a shred of doubt, oil was at the heart of it, not spreading democracy or "defending our freedoms."

In Florida, in late August, the grieving American father of a twenty-year-old Marine who died at Najaf set fire to a Marine vehicle to protest his son's death in this senseless war, and then he set himself on fire. The cocktail of grief and anger and desperation that would lead to such an act is not unique to this war. For many it was reminiscent of Buddhist monks self-immolating in the streets of Saigon forty years earlier.

Such an act is more than an expression of personal despair; it is a public act, a political statement of the most extreme kind, which by its nature relies on the will of others to respond. Thus it becomes even more tragic when it fails to penetrate what Thomas Hardy called the "blinkered mind" in his poem

"I Looked Up from My Writing," which portrays similarly tragic indifference to the similarly reckless pursuit of another war.

On Line at the Post Office

"All that is needed is that a state of war should exist."
—George Orwell, *1984*

Wait Here

The line stretches from the glass doors across the lobby to the sign. A day that begins with momentum, energy, purpose, now dissolves in the ether of Kafkian space-time. A few shuffle unpostaged mail. Others watch traffic pass outside. People going places. In motion. Out there. Unlike here. One man chatters cryptically into a cell phone. A young mother struggles with restless children. And the woman who now steps up to the counter is, I realize, sending a box to a soldier. After a year of sending packages to Iraq and another to Afghanistan, I know the signs. The customs form in sextuplicate flutters in one hand. Its dense print ominously warns of a possible phytosanitary inspection. The letters APO are scrawled on her box. Fatigue and urgency have drained her face. Maybe I have a similar look. I feel instantly connected, find myself calculating

On LIne at the Post Office

whether I'll be done in time to catch up with her.

My box contains canned soup, canned chili, power bars, beef jerky, vitamins, canned fruit, canned vegetables, canned tuna, toothbrushes and floss, and magazines. Mostly food. Heather had read that MREs don't provide enough calories for foot-soldiers in the mountains. And taste so bad soldiers carry Tabasco sauce to splatter on everything. They also mix bizarre combinations: dried creamer, instant cocoa, and crackers for S'mores. Pork and beans and jam? Here's a weird factoid: MREs are purposely short on fiber so soldiers don't get the shits in the middle of a firefight.

Francis is somewhere in eastern Afghanistan in the mountains that border Pakistan. In the Korengal Valley, I learn later, the so-called "Valley of Death" – a rugged landscape of tangled trees and barren mountains I swoop through regularly on Google Earth, wondering where he is in the forests and slopes of my satellite view.

A postal clerk once told me that with delivery confirmation I could be sure he received his package.

In the Afghan mountains?!

Yes, he assured me with a sturdy nod.

I imagined a postal carrier scurrying up the mountainside, bag on his shoulder, scanning the item and asking Francis to sign for it as he ducked incoming fire between rounds.

I paid the extra fee just to prove the clerk wrong but never bothered taking the unconfirmed receipt back to show him.

Few Americans have any personal stake in these wars.

Their mail has nothing to do with war.

Standing on line – there's always a line – I imagine other

postal customers going off to their next errands in the congested-shopping plazas all around the post office, off to Home Depot, Wal-Mart, the hair salon, the car wash. Picking up where they left off after Waiting Here. Back in September 2001, our leaders told us to shop. Shopping would save us. Shopping was patriotic. We embraced this patriotism.

Sometimes people told me – and probably the lady at the counter, too – thank him for his service. They were sincere. They meant well. But now, after years of war, and with so little sacrifice by so many and so much by so few, phrases like that resonate in the hollow white noise of bumper-sticker platitudes that have become the background chorus of our lives.

Our language has been damaged, our ability to express ourselves crippled by simplistic thinking, false equivalencies, truthiness. By war. Perhaps such expressions are a distillation of sorts, all we can say as we stand in the rubble of chaos and distortions that have brought us to this moment, the result finally, as Doris Lessing writes in *The Golden Notebook*, of "the thinning of language against the density of our experience." Our ability to respond is failing. Language itself is failing.

We are at war in Afghanistan, but not against Afghanistan, at war in Iraq, but not against Iraq. We're at war against Terror, which is neither a state nor a country nor a people. We live in an Orwellian hallucination in which war exists for its own sake, or to provide some warped sense of stability, or to preserve power for the powerful and make money for the moneyed.

War has become a natural force.

Who can argue with the wind? debate a hurricane or tornado?

On LIne at the Post Office

The case for war has been made – for generational war, for endless war. That we should always be at war is settled. Like winter. Like gravity.

By the time I reached the parking lot, the woman at the counter was gone. I would have liked to say hello, find out where her package was going, meet another military parent.

But I just headed home, where I tacked the customs receipt on my bulletin board along with dozens of others.

Off the Radar

IN MARCH 2006, WHILE Francis was in Afghanistan, Heather and I were interviewed by a reporter from the *Kansas City Star* named Malcolm Garcia. He'd seen a letter I wrote to the *Washington Post* about having a son serve in both Iraq *and* Afghanistan, and he wanted to do a feature article on that theme.

While Francis was deployed, I hadn't shied away from writing and speaking out against these wars and their conduct. My letter to the *Post* criticized the Bush administration for "its misguided policies, its campaign rhetoric and its chronic tendency to make bad decisions with tragic consequences"[1] – one of many such letters that also appeared in the *Kansas City Star* and *New York Times.* I regularly posted antiwar and anti-Bush articles – sometimes little more than rants, if I'm honest with myself – at progressive journals and blogs like *Counterpunch* and *Buzzflash*. I even appeared on National Public Radio. So I welcomed Garcia's query. I wanted to bring whatever attention we could to these wars.

---

1 "American Lives, Valued and 'Wasted,'" *Washington Post*, Jan. 10, 2006.

But this was something different for Heather. Her fears for Francis while he was overseas and her anger about the Administration's lies and bad policies were personal and private, painfully felt in the tenebrous depths of motherhood. Exposure might only worsen that pain. People would ask more questions, probe; sometimes for no other reason than to satisfy their own gratuitous curiosity. It would mean talking about things that were kept close, where emotional order, though fragile, was better managed.

But she courageously decided that exposure *was* the thing. *We* didn't matter any longer; this wasn't about us. It was about the wars, about bad policy, and most of all about the fact that these wars were so remote from the lives most people around us were leading in our insulated suburban world that no one seemed to care that we were at war, or if they did, it was often perceived in some anamorphic version of fighting "the terrorists" or waging "the war on terror," whatever that meant. Soldiers are heroes, yes, but the lawn needs mowing and we have to go to the mall.

"Even 'off the radar,' perils, fears persist" was the headline an editor planted atop Garcia's article in the *Star*.[2] "Off the radar" would have been fine with me. In fact, it's what I said in the interview. But what did *Even* even mean? The whole point was that it was *all* off the radar. There was no *Even* about it. The piece tends toward the melodramatic, perhaps the result of Garcia's literary stylings distilled by the verbal parsimony of his editor. Hearth, kitchen table, nighttime shadows – the moody stage setting for the interview: "Outside, nothing interrupts the evening except

---

2 Malcolm Garcia, "Even 'off the radar,' perils, fears persist," *Kansas City Star*, March 30, 2006, A1, 13. Print.

the soft glow of porch lights and the extended shadows beyond."

Francis – and vicariously we – were emblematic of an issue that had received little attention. In the professional (i.e., non-conscript) Army of these wars ("the Army you have ... not the Army you might want"), soldiers were now being deployed on multiple tours to both war zones. In fact, during his five years of active duty, Francis was *only* deployed twice, once each to Iraq and Afghanistan, while by 2006, when our *Star* interview took place, some were already on their third tour, with more yet ahead.[3] And these were compounded by stop-loss extensions, which entitled the Army to keep soldiers whose active duty tours expired in a war zone as long as their units remained there. All of this "off the radar."

Garcia's pathway into this issue was through the microcosm of our lives. He noted small details – that we wrote questions on a pad before going to bed because when Francis called at 3:00 a.m., we were too groggy to remember what we wanted to ask; that we kept notes and journal entries of those conversations because we had good reason to believe each one might be our last; that a friend of Heather's told her, "I can't stand listening to the news," so she didn't. The woman had no one in her family enlisted or deployed, so she avoided news about the wars. They were off her radar, and so were we.[4]

---

3 Ann Scott Tyson, "Repeat Iraq Tours Raise Risk of PTSD, Army Finds," *Washington Post*, December 20, 2006. Web: http://www.washingtonpost.com/wp-dyn/content/article/2006/12/19/AR2006121901659.html. Mark Sappenfield, "US troops weigh impact of stress: Some say repeated tours in Iraq could be a factor in recent murder allegations," *The Christian Science Monitor*, July 12, 2006. Web: https://www.csmonitor.com/2006/0712/p01s01-usmi.html.

4 On a plane trip in 2016, I overheard a veteran seated nearby telling a woman that he'd been deployed to a combination of Iraq, Afghanistan, and Somalia ten times. The woman responded that she couldn't stand listening to news about the wars on TV.

But "the news" seemed more obsessed with reality shows than wars, anyway.

"I've noticed," Heather said, that "with [Francis] going to Afghanistan, there's a real disconnect. There isn't any news." Or for sure, we had to search for it.

The data on news coverage bears this out. The Pew Research Center for Journalism and Media found, for example, that in January 2007 Afghanistan wasn't even ranked among the top ten stories for overall news coverage, including on-line, cable, and network TV, and only hit the number ten spot for print news.[5]

We were more than just worried; we were angry. It wasn't only us. Tens of thousands of families were experiencing these wars up close, sustaining terrible consequences – for thousands, the ultimate consequence of war – while for millions they didn't exist. We were willing to expose our fears in the hope of making ourselves representative, perhaps bringing more attention, which we hoped – foolishly, perhaps – would bring about change.

"This time it was Afghanistan," Garcia wrote. "At least it's not Iraq, well-meaning people tell them."

Back in January 2003, when Francis boarded the train for

---

5 "Democrats in Congress Top the Week's News," Pew Research Center, Jan. 8, 2007. Web:http://www.journalism.org/2007/01/08/pej-news-coverage-index-dec-31-2006-jan-5-2007/. By December 2009, Afghanistan finally made it into the rankings, though still hovering between just 2 and 5 percent of coverage and losing out to stories on the infamous Balloon Boy, a jet plane overshooting a Jamaican runway, the "Holiday Season," and by magnitudes, the healthcare debate, which captured 27 percent of coverage that month. See "Health Care Coverage Dominates the News," Pew Research Center, December 28, 2009. Web: http://www.journalism.org/2009/12/28/health-care-coverage-dominates-news/.

Fort Drum – soon, we then thought, to deploy to Afghanistan – we naïvely believed that at least he wouldn't be going to Iraq. The invasion of Afghanistan just months earlier seemed smaller, more focused, contained, and importantly for us, it also seemed just. It wasn't really an invasion, after all, we thought; it was a manhunt. That's where Francis's company, his entire battalion, in fact, was headed and what they'd trained for. But now, while we spoke with Garcia 2006, conditions in Afghanistan were even worse than Iraq; the threat, as I'll describe in another essay, was relentless; and the rationale dubious.

'No, We're Not from Texas'

Two soldiers stand at center court. Both wear olive camo BDUs, desert tan boots, and black berets. The flouncy beret, the trademark cap of French intellectuals and Latin American revolutionaries. Surely the most unlikely of head coverings for American soldiers, who sculpt and crease them into unnatural shapes, with crisp peaks in front and draped tightly on one side. The unintended, almost comical, result betrays a fundamental discomfort with the beret, though these two men do not seem uncomfortable in theirs, nor would they think there was anything funny about them. Both are officers. One leans slightly toward the other, his weight on one foot, a confident stance but less than a swagger. A man with nothing to prove. They talk, look around, point to an open doorway in the rear and along the striped blue mats that protect the varnished floor, plotting out the entrance of the incoming formation and routine to follow.

A company of soldiers will soon march in, just hours off the plane that brought them from Bagram Air Force Base in eastern Afghanistan by way of Kyrgyzstan to the north, where an old

Soviet Union air base has been converted to American use, and then through Germany, and finally here, to Fort Drum, New York. Less than forty-eight hours ago Francis and the others in this company had been in a battle zone. He was at his fire base until the penultimate day of a sixteen-month tour and told me later he was amazed at how fast things went once they pulled out and headed home. While he and the others awaited their flight, they were called to formation to honor the first three casualties from their replacements as the caskets passed before them, also going home.

The gymnasium stands are full and anticipation high. Children are restless. A few scamper about on the wide open floor. The band straggles in and sets up. Beneath the uniforms they're still musicians. A sax player warms up with some jazz riffs, while a horn player teases the opening bars of "Over the Rainbow," which he repeats several times with asides to another musician in between, explaining something, playing to illustrate a point. The melancholy notes resonate sweetly in the hollow of the gym. Ballads have a way of finding your softest emotional spot. The stands hum with chatter and laughter. Suddenly a woman darts across the floor. "I saw him!! I saw him!!" Applause. Nearby, others turn the pages of *The Year in Review*, a magazine we'd been given at the door along with a small American flag. Two people quietly read the last four pages, where the names and photos of those lost in this deployment appear.

'No, We're Not from Texas'

This was the second homecoming Heather and I attended in McGrath Gym at Fort Drum. The first was three years earlier, following a year-long tour in Iraq. We sat in nearly the same seats that night, close to the band, but high up in the stands at eye-level with the narrow balcony track around the perimeter. The railing was decorated with the flags of all the companies in the division. The words *10th Mountain Division (LI)*[1] glowed in gold letters on a blue field along the track facing. Posters proclaimed the division's motto: "Climb to Glory." My photos from that night are at nearly the same angle as our later visit, but that's where the similarities end.

We'd flown into Syracuse three days ahead of the Iraq ceremony in 2004, our first homecoming, uncertain which day he'd return and knowing no one from his company, soldiers or family members. Fort Drum is in northern New York State – the North Country, it's called – just outside of Watertown, about sixty miles north of Syracuse and only thirty miles or so from Canada. The hotels in Watertown were full, so we had to take a room in Syracuse. We'd held off on buying plane tickets because the company's arrival date was a moving target. For security reasons the Army doesn't even inform families about troop movements until the last minute, so we had to guess, balancing the risk of missing the ceremony against the high cost of last-minute tickets, or perhaps arriving early only to find out we had days to wait. We took the cautious and less expensive option, and sure enough, soon after we arrived the day was pushed back. We extended our hotel room and rental car and changed our return flights. So

1 Light Infantry

much for saving money. But we were long past thinking about costs; it really didn't matter. We would be there when the soldiers marched in. Heather, a special education teacher, was docked two days' pay for the extra time off, and as if unsatisfied with that penalty, her school district also deducted the pro-rated cost of her benefits for those two days. The gouge in that month's paycheck was startling.[2]

As the early dusk of September darkened the corridor of trees that enclosed the highway, we drove north on I-81 to Fort Drum that evening in 2004. The flight wouldn't arrive until late. We ate dinner at a Cracker Barrel near the post, dismayed to learn the restaurant closed at 10 p.m. We hadn't seen any place that would be open later, at least no place a soldier could take his mother. Our night was just beginning. With nowhere else to go, we went on to the North Gate and wove through a maze of concrete barricades at the checkpoint. The parking lot at the gym was deserted and the building locked. We'd been told at the gate that the flight wasn't expected until about 3 a.m., so we waited there for almost six hours, wondering if we were in the right place and if anything had changed. Every so often headlights whooshed past on the black road, but there were no other signs of life.

Sometime after midnight, a security vehicle appeared and MPs arranged wooden barricades around the parking (a good sign, we thought). Later another vehicle appeared and rearranged

---

[2] A year later Heather appeared before the school board with a packed house behind her and spoke to this issue so that no other teacher would have to incur such a penalty. A couple of board members were spotted subtly dabbing at tears. She got a rousing ovation from the gallery, and the policy of dinging teachers for personal days to attend military homecomings was blotted from the books (as if it had never happened).

'No, We're Not from Texas'

the barricades, now fencing us in (better or worse? – now we didn't know).

After they'd gone I silently weighed a question that had pressed on me, so to speak, for some time and could wait no longer – whether to relieve myself in the shrubs. I sized up the foliage. Heather worried that we'd get tossed off the post if I was seen.

(Didn't seem an issue for her. How *did* she do it?)

I continued studying the woods.

Mercifully, a light glowed as a door opened.

Inside, the gym was bright and busy with soldiers preparing to greet the Iraq group. A young sergeant asked, "Why are you waiting out there, sir? You and your wife can come inside if you want." I was too embarrassed to tell him we'd been out there for hours. He pointed down the hall to the men's room.

Back at the car, I shared the news with Heather, who was grading papers in the dim light. We continued our vigil and another hour passed. Then a truck roared by, coming from the direction of the airfield and loaded with what I guessed (correctly, it turned out) were piles of rucksacks from the incoming company. Now, as if some telepathic signal had gone out, a parade of vehicles appeared and came to a halt at the barricades. A woman climbed out of the lead SUV, moved a barricade aside, and the parade followed her into the parking lot. Whatever the MPs had in mind for parking, a wooden saw horse wasn't about to keep this woman out. It was nearly 3 a.m. Families poured out of the cars. Children bounced and giggled. Everyone filed into the bright gym, where a soldier at the door handed out flags.

A gaggle of wives with children sat near us, clutching Mylar balloons and posters. A couple might have been barely out of high school. They all lived on the post or in the sprawl of apartment buildings surrounding Fort Drum, and they'd waited a year for this moment. Life is not easy here. Winter is long and harsh. Lake effect storms and arctic temperatures blow down from Canada and across the wide plain of Lake Ontario. A month's pay for a private or specialist, or even a non-commissioned officer, comes to about the cost of rent and groceries, and little else. Debt is rampant. Exhausted charge cards, payday loans, usurious interest payments, and occasional help from parents and in-laws are how many young military families survive. The combat pay and tax relief soldiers get for deploying into a war zone may end up paying down debt accumulated before the next deployment. One woman told me that after one more tour, she and her husband would be clear. He just had to deploy once more to Iraq or Afghanistan – now, with extended tours the norm, at least another fifteen months.

The band exploded into a John Philip Sousa march as if it was a sunny Independence Day. Outside, beyond the parking lot, the post was quiet and dark. Fort Drum is a large base, with hundreds of acres of dense forest, barracks, warehouses, and offices spread out along its confusing loops and woodlands. In the midst of the surrounding stillness, the building glowed with cheers and applause and the band playing, and all of it drifting into the night at this bizarre hour as the returning company marched in, four abreast, to stand at attention through speeches and recognitions, while family members searched out their soldiers in the formation.

He was gaunt and sallow when we found him as a joyful chaos flooded the court. Heather clutched him for so long that he finally looked resolutely at me over her shoulder as if to say, "What can I do?" But our joy was tempered by his pallor and weight loss and the glassy look in his eyes, as if whatever he'd lived through had drained some of the life from him each day, like a nineteenth-century patient after a doctor had "bled" him.

The year ahead was difficult. Crowds, noise, human moiling – these frightened and disturbed him. More on this later. The year that followed was difficult.

We went to Longway's, a diner a few miles from the post – a place the soldiers like, but where a bathroom visit jeopardized my appetite – and we sat for an hour in a booth. Then Heather and I drove the sixty miles back to Syracuse, a white-knuckle ride through sunrise and into rush hour. We collapsed at the hotel, at once exhausted and too wired to sleep, and when we finally did drift off, a business meeting down the hall awakened us for good. We slept through both legs of our flights home that day.

A neighbor walking her dog stopped one afternoon while I was mowing the lawn and asked about the service banner in front of my house – a single blue star on a field of white with a red border. My mother once told me that the only time she ever saw my grandfather weep was the day he hung a service banner in his front window after my uncle joined the Navy in World War II. Back then, on any given block, many homes displayed service banners. They were a familiar sight. A gold star is substituted for blue if the service man or woman is killed. According to custom, only the immediate family should display a service banner. My neighbor thought it meant we were from Texas.

―∞―

During Francis's deployments I took to writing letters to newspapers.

Having a soldier deployed to the Middle East gives you gravitas, after a fashion. Your letters might get printed (a few, anyway); a radio producer might respond to your email.

Only a thin sliver of the population shared in these wars. This was a frequent theme of my letters. Those who decided we should be at war had none of their own skin in the game. No one in the executive branch and only a handful of congressmen even had sons or daughters in the military at that time, and not one had a soldier in Iraq or Afghanistan.

Another theme was Bush & Co. More of a general topic. Or target. The hypocrisy, cronyism, wrong-headedness, chuckle-headedness – and the relentless drumbeat of "stay the course" as a meme, even as Iraq quickly turned from seeming triumph into an avalanche of disasters that had only begun to tumble down on us.

One of my letters to the *New York Times* appeared on June 30, 2004, our thirtieth wedding anniversary. "Plunging poll numbers finally drove President Bush to make a speech about our disastrous

'No, We're Not from Texas'

adventure in Iraq," I wrote, "and what did he offer by way of explanation? Another version of the campaign stump speech that deceptively conflates the terrorist attacks of 9/11 with our war in Iraq."

Not exactly an anniversary card lyric.

As that year's election approached, I responded to a *Times* editorial by William Safire about one of the presidential debates: "Safire's praise for President Bush's performance in the second presidential debate seems a stretch at best. With the bar set as low as it was for the president, a victory is now measured by his ability to control his facial expressions and to pronounce the president of Poland's name correctly."

Snark (and cringe-worthy prose) came easily in the toxic political atmosphere of that year.

I wrote dozens of letters, sent most of them, and (mercifully) only saw a few make it into print. Editors heard from me a couple of times a week. More than once they saved me from myself.

And then there was NPR, where I gained the exalted status of Commentator, in which capacity I criticized, for all the nation to hear on *All Things Considered,* the epidemic of yellow ribbon magnets on cars and SUVs.

"Support the Troops!" they said. But what did that mean? I asked. They had an angry look. They weren't about "the Troops," but about politics, I declared. "Support the war!" they should say. "Support Bush!"

The right-wing blogosphere caught fire.

"Hey Sommer – Shut the F*ck [*sic*] up and just support the troops," one blogger shrieked at The Internet, though not without enough good taste to self-censor his language.

Predictably, some also went after NPR for broadcasting a "traitor-lover angst piece in the face of victory in Iraq!"

Victory? It'd been two years since the mission in Iraq had been "accomplished."

A gun club in Georgia wanted my address.

Conservative radio bloviator Michael Medved called me a "moonbat."

Sean Hannity's office at Fox News wanted an interview.

No, they wanted a piñata.

No, thank you.

Digital drool seeped through my computer screen.

Dissent, even doubt, was treason.

The mob was at my door. I imagined a Fox News truck rolling up on my lawn. My neighbors out there with pitchforks & torches – though I doubt they had either in their garages.

"Barbaric yawps," Whitman might have called my outcries.

An angry parent howling at the wind.

Willy Loman on the heath.

—⚔—

Rain spritzed through an overcast morning as we drove east through flyover America and then crossed the state line onto the New York State Thruway. We hadn't driven through this region in decades. We'd both grown up in New York, attended state schools, knew the landscape, but now it was all new again. A homecoming in more ways than one.

Hours later, as the North Country skies cleared into a warm, humid June evening, we searched out Carmen's apartment on a narrow street in the nests of on-post apartments and duplexes at Fort Drum. Carmen was our "call-out group" leader, a warm, cheerful woman with a shy little boy of about three. Her husband wouldn't be on tonight's flight, but still she was gathering her group to celebrate. First Lady Michelle Obama later recognized Carmen Blackmore on *The Oprah Winfrey Show* for her work with soldiers' families, "helping other families adjust," Mrs. Obama said, "delivering bad news and being there for other spouses when their husbands are away. So she's shouldering, in addition to her own burden, and this is typical. This is typical of our military families – holding it together, making it happen."

The entire brigade had been returning over the past three weeks – 3,200 men, arriving in waves from a sixteen-month, extended deployment in Afghanistan as seats on chartered planes came available.

The apartment was close, cluttered, busy with people crowding into the living room and spilling out onto the front lawn, a space about the size of a single-bay garage. One couple from Virginia wore matching T-shirts silk-screened with their son's basic training photo, a glum face, with his utility cap pulled low and the flag behind him. They smoked cigarettes from the same pack and candidly shared their son's troubles with self-discipline and school, troubles they hoped the Army would solve. I talked sports with a reticent teenager from Chicago whose brother was arriving tonight. He wanted to get a plate of food but was afraid of losing his shady lounger seat to his sister, who was biding her time in the glare of the late afternoon sun until he moved.

Cigarette smoke drifted through the air. Wives from nearby apartments arrived with food platters and extra chairs. In the driveway next door an SUV's rear window was soaped with the words "My Dad will be home in 7 days" – the number in the box to be updated daily. Carmen made frequent announcements about the plane's status. A man from Tennessee prodded chicken on the grill, while his wife reminded everyone to thank the Lord for being here, for the weather, for the incoming flight.

Cross-currents swirled all around us.

Black and white, conservative and liberal, religious and not-so-much – all shared the anticipation of the plane's arrival and the quiet profound joy of being part of this community at this moment. The arriving soldiers had survived while others had not, a reality that swept through on its own current. The casualty list on the back page of our Sunday paper carries the unprinted stories of all the families who do not attend homecoming ceremonies.

Characterizing these wars is difficult when you're looking outward from the isolated places where those who fight them live, when you're among families directly touched by them. The anger I carried about the policies that brought us here was subdued in the quiet warmth of the gathering. All that mattered right now was talking sports with a teenager, eating potato salad, losing myself in the serene hum of the moment.

In this war – these wars (it is one of the peculiarities of our times that I have to keep correcting the noun to a plural) – coffins return that no one sees; homecoming ceremonies take place in the middle of the night; catastrophic global events resulting in hundreds of thousands of deaths and displacing millions unfold, but a tap of the remote makes it all disappear. Invisibility is one such characteristic, even a defining condition of these wars.

Unlike World War II, which brought rationing, Victory Gardens, and ubiquitous service banners; or the Cold War, in which every child in America learned how to duck and cover; or Vietnam, when the draft could reach indiscriminately into almost any home (notably, not George W. Bush's or Donald Trump's), the wars we're now fighting allow many the option of indifference. President Bush urged Americans to carry on with life as usual after 9/11, to go shopping, he said – on its surface a bid to affirm normality and recharge a weakening economy and cratering stock market. But shopping may be the ultimate metaphor for how these engagements affect (or don't) most Americans, who can choose how much war to consume, and which flavor they prefer – color-guard-at-football-game, yellow-ribbon-magnet, tearful-"God-Bless-America" (am I the only one who's ever wondered why there's no comma after God, as in "God, bless America," in the imperative voice, letting the Big Guy/Gal in the Sky know who's blessed and who's damned?) – and leave the rest on the shelves. Sacrifice optional. Support for the wars has, in fact, largely depended on muting their impact. In a weird irony, the absence of sacrifice and charade of "normalcy" – of carrying on as if the attacks had no impact on American life, of making no changes in behavior – are how citizens are supposed to contribute to the strategic effort. Apathy as activism. Oxymoron as motto. But charade soon morphed into reality.

Heather and I became myopic because so much had to be filtered out. Our nerves were raw. A strange car in the driveway could be driven by a soldier in a Class-A uniform who would momentarily appear at our door with an envelope, or it could be someone turning around. Focusing on what had to be done in each moment, just that moment – jobs, chores, writing a letter to Francis, packing Christmas boxes for the squad – offered relief from fear, anger, anxiety. But the noise from beyond echoed in our tunnel, full of absurd contrasts to the narrow reality in which we lived. The legal wrangling over *Playboy* model Anna Nicole Smith's estate, Paris Hilton's latest escapades, who would be the next *American Idol* – these seemed far more pressing than wars raging in two countries. We tumbled around in an Orwellian nightmare like clothes in a dryer. Victory Gin flowed through the TV cable. Ignorance was adulated and knowledge belittled. Sentence fragments and gibberish held more sway than coherent syntax and facts. Our leader was elected because he's a guy you'd like to have a beer with, so the polls said. But he sounded like a schoolyard bully when he conducted what passed for international diplomacy.

Shopping would save us.

Apathy, we came to realize, and not terrorism, was the gravest danger we faced.

It is a commonplace that soldiers ultimately aren't fighting for a cause or policy; they're fighting for each other, for themselves, fighting to come home alive. An election was just around the corner, but no one talked politics at the barbeque.

As we sit in the stands at McGrath Gym awaiting the company from Afghanistan, Heather chats with a woman who's come to meet her husband. She's here alone and has been on her own most of the year. She wears a bright and colorful new dress and looks as fresh as if it's 5:00 in the evening and not 3:00 in the morning. I page through *The Year in Review* and find the photos of men from Francis's company whose families we'd sent sympathy cards to during the past year. The first time I've put faces to these names. Imagining Francis's face here comes all too easily. We received a few thank you notes, which came like gentle tugs from the far end of the fragile threads that connected us. I had to buy three cards on one occasion. It was unsettling just handing them to the clerk, who didn't seem to notice I was buying three sympathy cards at once as she bagged them. It seemed like the sort of thing someone would notice, but she didn't.

Homeland

*Odysseus awoke out of his sleep in his native land.
Yet he knew it not after his long absence ....*
　　　　　　　　　　The Odyssey, Book XIII
　　　　　　　　　　(trans. A. T. Murray)

"Pᴇᴏᴘʟᴇ ᴅᴏɴ'ᴛ ᴋɴᴏᴡ!"

His voice was breathless, weepy. Desperate.

Mustn't fall into his cadences, let him hear me panicking too.

"What happened?"

"They don't know!"

He'd been trying to call. Why didn't I pick up? Where was I?

Out. Forgot my phone.

Incomprehensible to a twenty-four-year-old. Forgetting your phone. But it's what I did. Went out. Forgot my phone.

Where was he?

On a highway overpass watching semis roar under his feet and measuring when to let go? Grasping a weapon in the other sweaty hand? He'd talked about getting a gun when he got out of the Army but never did. Not that I knew of. There came a point when Heather and I felt justified in going through his closet and drawers. We never found one, then or later.

No traffic noise. In fact, no noise at all. He was supposed to be at work.

"Where are you?"

At the restaurant, the Classic Cup, a Kansas City landmark. Everyone who lives here knows the Classic Cup, a Euro-style bistro on the Country Club Plaza. He made lunch for Roger Daltry there – twice, on separate concert tours. The second time, Daltry asked to meet Francis.

He mostly liked working there. He could be creative, invent recipes, stir up new salad dressings, christen an entrée with whatever name came to him. One time, when he knew Heather and I would be stopping in with some friends, I opened the menu and found a dish named after my first novel. Couldn't stop looking at the menu, like a teenager checking his hair in the mirror.

Mostly, I say, because the owner was a chiseler. Francis's paychecks were sometimes short. Still, he made friends there – the entire restaurant staff turned out for his wake. But restaurants are harsh places to work, and the Classic Cup was no exception.

He'd gone down to the wine cellar, which doubled as a dining room for private parties. I'd eaten dinner there and knew the room. Right now it was vacant and dark. He was alone. He'd been drinking. The wine cabinets would be locked, so not from the stock. Upstairs, it was full throttle Saturday night on the Plaza. The restaurant was busy, the kitchen chaotic. He'd be missed.

"They don't know!"
He said he felt like he was going to explode.
What don't they know?

Francis left for Basic Training at Fort Benning, Georgia, in May 2002 and returned home after five years of active duty in September 2007. For good, he hoped. We all did. But even while he was still in Afghanistan, with the end of his tour in sight, he worried about being sent back to Iraq and then stop-lossed again once he got there. And now that he was home, he had the Individual Ready Reserve dangling over him as the wars raged on.

Part of the deal for his initial enlistment bonus: four years of IRR following active duty. To all appearances civilian-wise he was done, but his status — as it was for thousands of soldiers — was technically "inactive." Could be called up any time for a "state of emergency," vague language that meant whatever the White House or Pentagon wanted it to mean in the endless and undefined stew of the so-called Global War on Terror. The IRR spawned a cottage industry of Army recruiters who could earn their points by re-enlisting soldiers like Francis to active duty or even the National Guard. He was the ideal candidate: fully trained, experienced, still in good physical condition, and possibly floundering in the civilian world of no-war. The invisible wounds, physical and moral, from two tours were simply ... invisible. Recruiters besieged him for the next three years after he returned home. Could be called up any time, they reminded him, as if he ever forgot. Business cards with cheery regrets – *Sorry I missed you, Frank!* – appeared in the slit at the front door. Sorry, indeed. The calls and emails were incessant. Won't get a heads-up, they warned. Just one day you'll get a call and that'll be it. Could be sent anywhere. *Even back to boot camp!* But if you re-enlist now you'll get another bonus, your choice of jobs. Life will be good! The memes of 1990s beer commercials found new life. (One persistent young recruiter came by the house a week or so after we buried Francis and had the misfortune of sharing his good cheer with me when I opened the door.)

But Francis wasn't buying. In a calculus based more on intuition than numbers, he amortized the bonus from his first enlistment, now divided by five years of training and deployments; ferocious heat, ubiquitous sand, tenacious camel spiders, and week after week of killing in Iraq; and then more killing in Afghanistan's rugged eastern mountains plus a stop-loss extension, hardships of every sort, firefights by the score, and memorial services for lost friends. The dollar value of a check that once seemed like a fortune to a wide-eyed eighteen-year-old had been eroded by the inflation of all he'd lived through in five long years, and now too, by the lingering injuries he quietly endured.

Unlike many recruits, he'd held on to most of his original bonus money and added to it while he was in the Army. Overseas deployments boosted pay and lowered taxes and expenses. I helped him build up a small basket of CDs at his credit union while he was deployed. Back at Fort Drum he lived in the barracks rather than take an apartment off-post. He would tell us about other "kids," as he called them, showing up in shiny new trucks and sports cars. Bonus money and deployment pay uncorked like a shaken bottle of cheap champagne. While it didn't come close to the sticker price of a new F150 or Charger, it was enough for a down payment. But now, back home on regular pay and with no more bonus money on the horizon, they could only watch as their gleaming vehicles were towed away within the year. Few realized this was part of the dealer's business plan – to have a nearly new car up for resale a year later while banking the down payment and whatever heavy interest he could collect until the car returned to his lot like a lost dog finding its way home. Francis had already been rung out in this cycle before he enlisted. At barely eighteen, and with little income and no credit history, he'd found a shady car dealer to sell him a truck on credit at an interest rate that would have made a payday lender blush. Then, inevitably, a few months later he found himself behind on the payments. Going into the service had helped clear him of a bad debt and a bad decision, if not the bad memory of watching a tow-truck operator with an attitude haul his truck away.

Despite the relentless media thrum to the contrary, for many enlistment wasn't a matter of patriotism but of desperation. The former just varnished the latter with an appealing shine. For every Pat Tillman who joined up from a consuming sense of patriotic zeal following the 9/11 attacks, there were scores who'd hit a dead end in life. Francis shared stories of kids from broken and abusive homes; who'd had scrapes (or more) with the law, marital troubles, academic failure, or were simply poor. One soldier's father told me, as we waited for the plane with our sons on board to return from Afghanistan, that his son had been in and out of trouble throughout high school and was headed nowhere afterwards. The boy, he said, was disruptive, impulsive, easily agitated, and had a short attention span. After school he couldn't keep a job and he'd run out of options. The man said he hoped the Army would "straighten him out," but he was worried about what to expect when his son arrived in a few hours. Later I asked Francis if he knew the kid. "Yeah," he huffed, "I thought he'd get somebody killed over there."

We've draped the billowing colors of patriotism on everyone who signs up, but the undraped reality tells another story – many stories. Pat Tillman became the face of pure unadulterated patriotism, a perfect-pitch morality tale on a grand scale. He sacrificed the big football contract for the national commonweal and then made the ultimate sacrifice in Afghanistan, which the Army then glazed in its own tale of heroism, until the façade cracked and the reality of his death under friendly fire was revealed. While there is nothing unheroic about such a death in combat, the story now seemed to want an asterisk. It was less than ideal for marketing purposes, so the Army's public relations folks cooked up another version and worked it like folded dough into a national myth until the Tillman family learned the truth not only of their son's death but of how it had been cravenly used to market this sanitized brand of patriotism. "After it happened," Tillman's father, Patrick Tillman, Sr., said, "all the people in positions of authority went out of their way to script this. They purposely interfered with the investigation. They covered it up. I think they thought they could control it, and they realized that their recruiting efforts were going to go to hell in a hand basket if the truth about his death got out. They blew up their poster boy."[1] He was even less diplomatic writing to Brigadier General Gary M. Jones, who signed off on the findings when the Army concluded its investigation: "Fuck you ... and yours."[2]

Tillman was only a few weeks behind Francis in Basic Training at Fort Benning. They and others breathed the same narcotic post-9/11 air – pure oxygen compared to the toxic fumes Francis had been inhaling for the year or so after he finished high school. But he'd run out of future. He knew he was in a bad place when he brought the recruitment brochures home.

—⁂—

The summer of 2007, when Francis finally returned home, was hot. Here in eastern Kansas, a heat wave that lasted for weeks saw the thermometer on our deck hit 104° and 105° Fahrenheit on consecutive days. Temps dipping into the 90s felt like a cold front blowing in from Canada. The heat wave was worldwide. Hungary saw a record temperature of 107° F.[3] Hundreds throughout Europe and Asia died in heat-related incidents and wildfires fueled by drought that summer.

[1] Josh White, "Tillman's Parents Are Critical Of Army," *Washington Post*, May 23, 2005. Web: http://www.washingtonpost.com/wp-dyn/content/article/2005/05/22/AR2005052200865.html
[2] Sam Stein, "Pat Tillman's Father To Army Investigator: 'F— You ... And Yours,'" *Huffington Post*, Aug. 12, 2010. Web: http://www.huffingtonpost.com/2010/08/12/pat-tillmans-father-to-ar_n_680128.html
[3] "Death toll rises in southern Europe's heatwave," *The Guardian*, 24 July 2007, http://www.theguardian.com/world/2007/jul/25/weather.travelnews.

A sense of catastrophe, of disaster, percolated through newscasts, websites, everyday conversation. The planet itself was shuddering, or so it felt, warning us that this volatile weather, from drought to floods, from wildfires and extreme heat to the exponential increase in tornados and mega-hurricanes, meant something. But too much money was at stake to ask if our addictions to fossil fuels and consumption had anything to do with it. If you were in Congress (or the White House), blithe, even willful, ignorance was preferable to admitting that climate scientists might be on to something. And if you worked for an oil company – or lobbied for one – your next promotion or bonus or even your job depended on finding some other explanation. Didn't matter what. As muckraking author Upton Sinclair declared, "It is difficult to get a man to understand something, when his salary depends on his not understanding it."[4]

But what could explain this chaos, this imminent sense that judgment was upon us?

The gays and atheists! That was it. So said televangelist Pat Robertson, who predicted that Judgment Day would arrive on April 29, 2007. But somehow the world lurched onward through that date. Whatever was going on seemed to be occurring in a national and global version of death by a thousand cuts. Even if Robertson's wacky and bigoted predictions had nothing to do with it, fools still managed to absorb more of our collective attention than voices of reason. We prefer spectacle to reality. Fundamentalism and jingoism are easy – understanding, edu-

---

4 Upton Sinclair, *I, Candidate for Governor: And How I Got Licked* (Pasadena: published by the author, 1935), p. 109.

cation, negotiation hard. I had once thought, naïvely, that 9/11 would precipitate the greatest conservation campaign this country had ever seen; that we'd downsize, conserve, cease and desist with the gas-guzzling, 68-degrees-inside-when-it's-102-outside mentality; that corrupt regimes in the Middle East would soon find that we didn't need their oil because ... we didn't need that much oil after all. We wouldn't drill-baby-drill here instead of importing oil; we'd just stop using so much. It would become unpatriotic, just plain uncool, to guzzle gas. The shopping orgasm we call Christmas might actually become the serene and peaceful season Hallmark and (bizarrely) beer commercials would have us believe it was. But no, I was wrong. Instead, America went on a shopping and driving and suburban sprawling binge that persists to this day. Humvees became status symbols for the driveway. You needed one for your mission to the mall. Francis, who'd driven his share of Humvees, would sniff in disgust when he saw one on the road at home.

There was more in 2007. That spring a Virginia Tech student with a pair of semi-automatic handguns went on a campus-wide rampage and killed thirty-two people before taking his own life. A bridge collapsed on a section of Interstate 35 in Minnesota, killing thirteen people and becoming an emblem of our collapsing infrastructure. And even as war raged in Afghanistan, where Francis had been deployed for over a year, 2007 was the worst year yet for American casualties in Iraq, with the number killed for that year alone reaching a new high at 899. More and more troops were being sent to Iraq: 20,000 in January; 7,000 in

March; another 12,000 in April.[5] By August total "coalition of the willing" deaths hit 4,000 since the invasion began, more than three-quarters of them American, while Iraqi civilian deaths were immeasurable because they were unmeasured.

When President Bush announced an escalation of the war in Iraq at the beginning of 2007, it was benignly, even upliftingly, captioned "The New Way Forward," a phrase that held out the promise of a Tony Robbins seminar packaged in a box of New Age herbal tea. Who could find fault with the prospect of a New Way Forward? What better way than New? The Administration seemed confident, too, that no one would wonder if the old way had been backward. Orwellian Newspeak and its substructure, Doublethink, now characterized the Administration's discourse. And when you pried it open, this new-agey New Way Forward package offered yet another lexical flavor inside: *troop surge*,[6] which sounded so much better – tidier, more contained, circumscribed – than *escalation*, a word that crackled with the resonance of another war that began like this one and then *escalated* in similar ways, with similar rationales packaged in similar language, and in the collective living memory of many, a similar outcome likely. The language of politics and war – a language of deception, to

---

5 "A Timeline of the Iraq War," *Think Progress,* March 17, 2006. Web: https://thinkprogress.org/a-timeline-of-the-iraq-war-6622633720be/
6 While President Barack Obama did not use that phrase in his 2009 speech at the U.S. Military Academy to announce that he was increasing by 30,000 the number of troops deployed to Afghanistan, the news media quickly dubbed it a "troop surge." As I listened to his speech, I couldn't help but think that if I was reading the text without knowing who gave it and when, I would have thought it was another Bush speech written by David Frum or Michael Gerson, both of whom, like Obama, tended to favor complete sentences. "Text: Obama's Speech on Afghanistan," CBS News, December 1, 2009. Web: http://www.cbsnews.com/news/text-obamas-speech-on-afghanistan/.

which we'd been subjected for years to rationalize these wars – had become a fixture in the climate of our discourse, trickling down, so to speak, into our daily interchanges and infecting even easy exchanges in workplace break rooms, over backyard fences, on checkout lines at the grocery store. If you weren't *with us*, you were *against us*. Don't say *escalation*, say *surge*. Don't say *invasion*, say *war*. And always refer to the enemy as *The Terrorists* – which fixed all, with the definitiveness of the definite article, from Iraq to Afghanistan to, essentially, the entire Muslim world (wherever Muslims may reside), in a direct lineage to the 9/11 killers. The oppression of heat waves and dire headlines and troop-surging war was evident everywhere: in American flag apparel that oozed with chip-on-the-shoulder anger and in the fear of confrontation that a simple usage might bring with it. Rush Limbaugh hyper-ventilated these memes into millions of ears through dashboards and kitchen radios. Ditto Fox News. Aggression and malignancy formed a thick verbal smog that churned up through the disasters of that year (and, it should be said, have only grown worse since then).

All of this was the cacophony, the white noise of our lives when Francis returned home in 2007. Anger was the dominant mood of America – an unfocused vitriol that found targets wherever it aimed, or didn't bother aiming, just blew scattershot in every direction, but mostly at immigrants, minorities, gays, the poor.

But TV also told us that by 2007 Americans were war-weary. This seemed odd since so few Americans had any direct connection to these wars. Many had shopped their way through them or spent whatever capital of time and energy they had on fantasy football and debating who'd survive *Survivor*. But some of this fatigue had also seeped over from the general chagrin that many in the military felt. A *New York Times*/CBS poll conducted that year among service members and their families revealed that two-thirds had become disillusioned with the war in Iraq and a majority did not think the U.S. should have invaded Iraq. Even among some of the most gung-ho military families, the sense of purpose had been drained. One mother, recounting a phone call from her son in Iraq, said, "There was no pride left in his voice, just this robotic sense of despair." Her son had just described killing women and children in the street. "We had no choice," he told her.[7]

We heard as much from Francis. The wars created a deep feeling of inner conflict: the policy's bad and the wars are wrong, yet here I am with these other men, surrounded by well-armed fighters who want to kill us, and I'm trained not only to survive but to prevail, and that's what I'll do until I get home. Odysseus in the mountains (or desert). The Iliad become the Odyssey. And while he was in the mountains, I was standing at a crossroads in Kansas City holding an antiwar sign for passing traffic, and he was fine with that, too. He didn't always believe the Iraq invasion had been wrong; he grew into it – or it grew into him like cancer. He'd once been proud that the 10th Mountain was the first Army division sent to Afghanistan in Operation Enduring Freedom, following the 9/11 attacks, though now, years later, the point of what they were doing

---

7 Ian Urbina, "As Loved Ones Fight On, War Doubts Arise," *New York Times*, July 15, 2007. Web: http://www.nytimes.com/2007/07/15/us/15protest.html?_r=0

there, among people who harbored Taliban fighters and whose village and clan leaders were often corrupt, seemed lost on him. "When you don't have a clearly defined mission," Bryan Casler, a Marine Corps rifleman, said, regarding the Iraq occupation, "the mission becomes to come home alive, to survive."[8] And such lack of purpose, Casler went on to say, leads to behaviors like defecating and urinating into MRE bags before tossing them to hungry Iraqi children.

Francis's battalion commander, Lieutenant Colonel Chris Cavoli, wrote an open letter to family members describing relations with villagers on the Afghanistan tour in 2006-7, perhaps sanding and smoothing the rough edges of reality for the sake of his audience:

> [T]he most important thing we do is stay out among the people and protect them. We are there with them. We are out in the rain and the sun and the wind, and we are in their villages and on their roads keeping the enemy away from them. And they know it. Over time, as the people have realized that we are there for them, that we truly are committed to our mission, they have come to trust us. They bring us food, they bring us 'chai,' and most of all they bring us information about the enemy. By being among them in the good times and the bad, we have earned their trust, and given them the confidence to side with us against the enemy.[9]

---

8 Iraq Veterans Against the War and Aaron Glantz, *Winter Soldier, Iraq and Afghanistan: Eyewitness Accounts of the Occupations* (Chicago: Haymarket Books, 2008), p. 79.
9 LTC Chris Cavoli, undated email to "Chosin Family," circa Sept. 2006.

Francis had a less glossy take. He described one instance in which an Army commander gave villagers a generator to provide electricity. The village elder then took the generator home and mounted it on top of his house like a cupola, where it remained unused, a symbol of his importance in the village because the Americans had given this thing to him and him alone.

The sense of entrapment in these seemingly endless wars and befuddlement over finding an answerable way out had a familiar ring. Comparisons to the Vietnam War had had been around since even before the invasion of Iraq. Many antiwar groups recognized the terrain and voiced opposition for many of the same reasons – the American over-reaction, the inevitable quagmire, the political motives that led to war and justified perpetuating it. The Kansas City Iraq Task Force, for instance, had been protesting U.S. sanctions against Iraq for several years before the invasion because of the hardships they imposed on Iraqi citizens. *New York Times* columnist Paul Krugman outlined the similarities between Vietnam and Iraq: "Gulf of Tonkin attack, meet nonexistent W.M.D. and Al Qaeda links. 'Hearts and minds,' meet 'welcome us as liberators.' 'Light at the end of the tunnel,' meet 'turned the corner.' Vietnamization, meet the new Iraqi Army."[10] Also writing for the *Times*, Frank Rich described Iraq as "Vietnam on speed – the false endings of that tragic decade re-enacted and compressed

---

10 Paul Krugman, "The Vietnam Analogy," *New York Times*, April 16, 2004. Web: http://www.nytimes.com/2004/04/16/opinion/16KRUG.html. See also Thomas E. Ricks, "For Vietnam Vet Anthony Zinni, Another War on Shaky Territory," washingtonpost.com, December 23, 2003. Web: http://work.colum.edu/~amiller/wpostzinni.htm. For Zinni's speech at Crystal City, see https://www.mca-marines.org/mcaToday/mca_today_0803.htm.

in jump cuts, a quagmire retooled for the MTV attention span."[11] But such comparisons were not only the provenance of antiwar activists and liberal columnists. As early as 2003, Marine Corps General Anthony Zinni reminded his audience that Vietnam was "where we heard the garbage and the lies," as he asked, regarding Iraq, "Is it happening again?" A former commander of the U.S. Central Command, Zinni was hardly throwing red meat to antiwar activists. Rather he was addressing military officers at the U.S. Marine Corps Association and Naval Institute Forum in Crystal City, a convention underwritten by corporate sponsors also notable for their disdain for the politically leftward, such as Northrop Grumman, Raytheon, Lockheed Martin, Bell Helicopter, and General Dynamics. Zinni's session was entitled "How Do We Overhaul the Nation's Defense to Win the Next War?" Regarding Iraq, the answer – in 2003 – was, Don't get sucked into it, as we did in Vietnam forty years earlier.

Francis's disdain for the wars, especially Iraq, was more than just a reflection of his parents' progressive attitudes. They were also shared by many of the nation's military leaders, who thought going into Iraq was a bad idea badly executed,[12] a notable contrast to the Pentagon's eagerness decades earlier to press for military solutions in Vietnam and even before that, notoriously, during

---

11 Frank Rich, "Forget Armor. All You Need Is Love," *New York Times*, Jan. 30, 2005. Web: http://www.nytimes.com/2005/01/30/arts/forget-armor-all-you-need-is-love.html.

12 Mark Sauer, "Generals Opposing Iraq War Break with Military Tradition," *San Diego Union-Tribune*, Sept. 23, 2007. Web http://legacy.utsandiego.com/news/world/iraq/20070923-9999-1n23generals.html. See also Erin Solaro, "Retired generals rising up against Iraq war," *Seattle Post Intelligencer*, April 15, 2006. Web: http://www.seattlepi.com/local/opinion/article/Retired-generals-rising-up-against-Iraq-war-1201001.php

the 1963 Soviet missile crisis, which likely would have ended in nuclear holocaust if the Joint Chiefs had had their way. For many of us who lived through those times, this was a startling turnabout that gave even greater credibility to those generals who opposed the war and their willingness to say so publicly. The earliest and most notable instance was General Eric Shinsecki, who on February 25, 2003, advised the Senate Armed Services Committee that "[s]omething on the order of several hundred thousand soldiers" would be needed if the U.S. decided to invade Iraq.[13] The Bush Administration's response was rapid and harsh. Deputy Secretary of Defense Paul Wolfowitz's tone suggested more than "reasonable confidence" two days later, when he snidely responded, "We can say with reasonable confidence that the notion of hundreds of thousands of American troops is way off the mark." The next day Rumsfeld himself, who'd either co-opted Wolfowitz's cliché or provided it, added, "The idea that it would take several hundred thousand U.S. forces I think is far off the mark." A year and a half later, Secretary of State (Ret. Gen.) Colin Powell came to Shinsecki's defense, sort of, when he observed of the tactical situation in Iraq, "We don't have enough troops. We don't control the terrain." For opponents of the war, Powell's ship of credibility had already sunk with his pre-invasion

---

13 "Army chief: Force to occupy Iraq massive," *USA Today*, Feb. 25, 2003. Web: http://usatoday30.usatoday.com/news/world/iraq/2003-02-25-iraq-us_x.htm.

U.N. presentation on aluminum tubes and WMD in Iraq, while for advocates, remarks like this only confirmed that his ship was at least floundering. But he wasn't the only one to say so. Coalition Provisional Authority advisor Larry Diamond told then National Security Advisor Condoleeza Rice in a 2004 memo, "In my weeks in Iraq, I did not meet a single military officer who felt, privately, that we had enough troops."[14] Shinsecki was marginalized and pushed out. Powell too.

Among those leading the so-called "Revolt of the Generals" was Major General Paul Eaton, who called for Rumsfeld to resign. With a bluntness we don't typically associate with military jargon, but a characteristically unsparing use of Latinate modifiers, Eaton said Rumsfeld "has shown himself incompetent strategically, operationally and tactically, and is far more than anyone else responsible for what has happened to our important mission in Iraq."[15] Retired Lieutenant General William Odom also seemed to be in search of language strong enough to state his concerns. Three years after Shinsecki's testimony, Odom appeared before the Senate Foreign Relations Committee on January 18, 2007, and told senators, "It is a strategic error of monumental proportions to view the war as confined to Iraq. Yet this is the implicit assumption on which the president's new strategy is based. We have turned it into two wars that vastly exceed the borders of

---

14 "Eric Shinseki on War & Peace," *On the Issues*, http://www.ontheissues. org/celeb/Eric_Shinseki_War_+_Peace.htm. G.B. Trudeau, *The War in Quotes* (Andrews McMeel, 2008), pp. 42-3; see also: http://www.ontheissues.org/ Doonesbury_Quotes.htm.
15 Paul D. Eaton, "A Top-Down Review for the Pentagon," *New York Times*, March 19, 2006. Web: http://www.nytimes.com/2006/03/19/opinion/19eaton. html?pagewanted=print&_r=0.

Iraq." He presciently added that even an invasion force exponentially larger than that which Rumsfeld and Bush tried to convince the public was needed only would "have delayed a civil war but could not have prevented it." He summed up his remarks by describing the war in Iraq as "the greatest strategic disaster in our history."[16] As of this writing, Iraq is imploding under a sectarian civil war, just as Odom predicted. But as one of W's advisors infamously noted, the Bush Administration was not part of "the reality-based community."[17] The Neocons got their war, and the country swirled into a vortex of déjà-vu-all-over-again as we slogged into yet another Big Muddy in the Big Sandbox, as soldiers called Iraq, that felt so familiar and so inescapable, and now, oddly, so different.

—∞—

On May 29, 2007, Cindy Sheehan gave up her vigil at the front gate of President Bush's ranch in Crawford, Texas. The poor woman was broken and broke. She only ever had one question for Bush: "What was the noble cause my son died for?" That's what brought her to Crawford and kept her at his front gate in sweltering heat, blazing sun, and sparse conditions for nearly a month. Beneath all of the political turbulence surrounding her was her grief, an emotion – no, a state of being – that, as much

---

16 Lt. Gen. William E. Odom (Ret.), "What Can Be Done in Iraq?" Text of testimony before the Senate Foreign Relations Committee, 18 January 2007. Web: http://www.antiwar.com/orig/odom.php?articleid=10396.
17 Ron Suskind, "Without a Doubt," *New York Times*, October 17, 2004. Web: http://query.nytimes.com/gst/fullpage.html?res=9C05EFD8113BF934A25753C1A9629C8B63.

as I sympathized with her, I did not fully understand until years later, when I realized that if Francis had been killed in Iraq that could as easily have been me in Crawford. My anger at Bush & Co. and all who supported him was that great. But Sheehan's question for Bush wasn't ultimately about her son or her grief – it was about the wars, and for all the contempt and outright hatred many on the right heaped on this grieving woman, her one question, in its simplicity, proved to be the most penetrating of any that were asked about Iraq. For a time, she was the face of all that was wrong with that war.

She was seldom off my radar in May. I even considered going to Crawford to join the protest there, but that month had been consuming at our house. Erin completed her junior year at the University of Kansas and moved home to begin a summer internship in journalism with a trade magazine. Alex, an ER nurse in a nearby hospital, had also been living here since the beginning of the year. His twelve-hour shifts were sometimes a slow-leak that drained our daily routines as we worked around his sleep and work schedule. For Heather, the end of the school year meant testing (ever more each year in the tyranny of an increasingly all-testing-all-the-time curriculm), grading, and closing out her room. All the while, she was deeply worried about her mother, Mary, whose leukemia had now ominously recurred. Heather made four trips to Florida that year and was now making arrangements to visit Mary again, while at the same time we anticipated Francis's return to Fort Drum from Afghanistan within weeks.

His birthday is May 12th. Mother's Day fell on the 13th that year. And Heather's birthday is the 14th. For her, an emotional bombshell exploding in slow motion over three days. He turned twenty-four – his second birthday in Afghanistan.

He called at 5:15 a.m. on Heather's birthday.

Five years of calls like this and they still startled us. Pens placed on nightstands were somehow drained of ink in the hours since we put them there. Notepads grew Teflon underbellies and slipped away as we scribbled while perched on the edge of the bed, phone cradled in a shoulder, head gasping for wakefulness

He was in Asadabad. Years later his friend Bobby told me that when the base commander saw the exhausted, battle-worn men in Combat Company after months in the eastern mountains, he snorted that they looked like prisoners of war. There were soldiers at Asadabad who'd never left the base, never been in combat, never fired a weapon at another human being or had one shoot at them. They wore clean uniforms, showered daily, watched TV, worked out in the weight room, emailed and Skyped with their families, and ate hot meals prepared by well-paid contract employees of companies like Halliburton subsidiary KBR three times a day. On TV at home, they got to be heroes too. The commander gave orders immediately to suspend use of the showers by anyone other than Combat Company soldiers. They could also go to the head of the line in the chow hall, which was now open 24-7 for them only, and have full use of computers, TVs, and rec rooms. In short, the base was at their disposal and everyone else should stand down for them.

Francis was expected to arrive at Fort Drum around June 12-15. I made reservations for New York, and for Heather's trip to be with her mother.

Our travel to Fort Drum for the homecoming ceremony that June was part of a bigger driving and camping trip that took us through upstate New York, Vermont, New Hampshire, Cape Cod, and then the long ride home to Kansas. We spent three days in New York's North Country with Francis, which had such exceptional weather that June that we even considered buying a retirement house in one of the small towns along the St. Lawrence Seaway. But the weather was exceptional and allowing the impulse to fade a good decision in more ways than we imagined.

Those early days and weeks after Francis returned were fine, in the full sense of the word. His relief at being back, eating well, showering and sleeping when he wished for as long as he wished seemed to give him a glow. He was on short-time for active duty and wouldn't be deploying again. He had two weeks of leave ahead, followed by another few weeks at Fort Drum late in the summer, and then he'd return home in September to restart life as a civilian. We lived in the moment, and he seemed genuinely grateful to spend time with us. The difference in his demeanor was pronounced – softer, quieter, always reaching to hold a door or carry items for us. He took care of paperwork and banking. We checked on his car, a Jeep that he'd left at a friend's place. It hadn't been started or moved in almost two years and ended up salvage. We visited Sackets Harbor, toured the colonial fort there, ate at a restaurant he liked. The next day we traveled north along the Seaway to Alexandria Bay for a picnic lunch by the water on possibly one of the finest and clearest days that town saw all year.

When Heather and I departed a few days later it was with the additional relief of knowing that the deployments were done and he'd be home soon. We drove to the Hudson Valley and spent several days seeing family and friends. Then on to the White Mountains, where we camped for two nights and shared our meals with squadrons of the biggest, nastiest mosquitoes we'd ever seen. Nightfall brought cooler temps and relief by the fire. We visited Franconia, where we saw the now-faceless remains of The Old Man of the Mountain, immortalized by Nathaniel Hawthorne in his short story "The Great Stone Face" and more recently a tune by Bill Staines, "Old Man of the Mountain." But the old man's craggy profile had crumbled in a rock slide a few years earlier, leaving a shadowy, flat silhouette like the end of a bread loaf on the mountainside and visitors to imagine the face that had been there for eons, and some to remember it. Robert Frost had lived for a time in a farmhouse in Franconia, so we took in the view of distant hills from his front porch and wandered the grounds, the only visitors that afternoon. His name appears in a rough scrawl on the rusted mailbox – *R. Frost* – and one of his poems is tacked on a telephone pole. We visited my folks in Cape Cod for a few days before turning west again for home.

Heather's mother had continued declining, so Heather left for Florida almost as soon as we'd unpacked the car, the last time she'd see her in a conscious state. Later that summer, in August, she wanted Francis to take a couple days of his final leave to go to Florida. It was near the end for Mary. There wouldn't be another chance. She'd been a generous grandmother to Francis and all of her grandchildren throughout their lives. But he mostly deflected the question until his leave was up. Heather was both hurt and angry, and it wasn't until years later, after we'd lost him, that she found peace in deciding that she perhaps didn't fully understand why going there now seemed less urgent to him.

He'd gained a callousness about death – at least on the surface. "Death is just something that happens," he said. "People die, you move on." Cold. His grandmother had worried constantly while he was overseas. She'd traveled to Fort Benning, Georgia, for his graduation from Basic Training and then to Kansas for the only Christmas he was home while in the service. Even now I think Francis was just lazy. It was too much hassle to go visit, and mostly would have been boring and depressing for him. It was a hurt that chafed Heather for years. It was, too, a reminder that for all the lionizing we do of soldiers in these wars, including my own son, the people who fight them are as flawed as those who don't. Heather finally decided that he only had the two weeks' leave, so maybe this was too much to ask. Mary passed away that November. Heather was with her that night, talking to her for hours before she died, certain her voice penetrated the coma's shield. And we all were there that Thanksgiving, Francis too, for an uncomfortable gathering, as Mary's husband Quimby followed the letter of her wishes: no memorial service. She wanted no one troubled about her passing. Chronically self-deprecating throughout her life, maybe she was even embarrassed about dying. So there was no service, and no proper closure to a life of eighty-some years, a note that I add here because in the time since we lost Francis the value of our services for him has spiraled outward as many new friendships emerged from meeting his friends. "Rituals matter," my friend Bill Decker told me just days after the service for Francis. Not religion, but ritual – the time taken, the gathering, the poems and eulogies and music, the meals shared, the stories, and even, weird as it felt at the time, the laughter. No, for Heather I'll say it, Francis should have made the effort to go, but then, so much is expected, there's so much pressure, and for many, coming home from these wars is the hardest part.

Home

He came home to autumn, which unfolded in cool easy days following a brutally hot summer. Easy from pure relief. He was here. We could breathe again – deep breaths, long breaths. Cool air. Un-Zeppelin-like easy cool air. We sat by a fire in the backyard and talked of nothing. We'd covered his plans before he arrived and would talk of them again soon. Leave that for now. Watch the flames, but don't look too deeply, as Melville warned. The warmth and crackle of the fire washed over us. Cool air and warm fire. Unfolded legs, untensed muscles, and heads, in perfect balance between cool and warm as peepers chirped in the woods beyond our fence and bats swooped overhead and lightning bugs tossed glitter over the yard.

All that came before had led to this moment.

These early weeks had their idyllic moments, but they were still just moments. Life stumbled on. After months of sorting through brochures and websites for culinary schools from Vermont to Colorado, beginning while he was still in Afghanistan, Francis announced that he'd attend nearby Johnson County Community College, which had a widely-acclaimed culinary program and a much lower price tag than the other schools.

And he'd live at home while he went to school.

Here? I lightly ventured. At home? As in, *our house?*

Erin was at college. Alex had been living here for over a year and had just (finally) found a place of his own. And Francis, we thought, would be somewhere close by, doing what he loved in a place where he wouldn't have to clean his weapon and hoist eighty pounds of gear on his back before he left his apartment and then worry about sniper fire once he shut the door behind him.

His apartment, we thought.

We were ready for a break. To be on our own. Yes, empty the nest – it's okay!

Fly, my pretties!

The house to ourselves, our own schedules, save money, walk around the house naked if we chose (not that we did, much), eat what we liked, and buy less of it, have the kitchen sink empty from time to time, give the washer and dryer time to cool off between loads, watch Masterpiece Theater instead of SportsCenter. At twenty-one years old, Erin was our youngest and would be at school for another year. Alex was twenty-eight, had a good job, and now his own place. And Francis – doomed to be the middle-child – was twenty-four, with the GI bill and his savings to take him through college. We'd earned this.

And did I mention expenses? He wanted to save money, he

said, but didn't say anything about pitching in so we could save ours, too.

For three years? I sputtered.

Yup, three-year program.

Oh.

Small voice. A whisper. A subtle nod of ... welcome.

And Heather?

We exchanged a glance.

This wasn't the plan.

He didn't pick up on the vibe. He'd already worked things out.

We didn't need to.

—⚜—

Of course, he'd want to be out with his friends. Go to barbecues and ball games, party. During the day he took care of business. School registration, meet with the veterans affairs officer at the college. He bought a car, a new phone, unpacked most of his stuff (some of the clutter never disappeared), got new clothes, joined a health club, checked in at the Kansas City VA for doctor appointments. He would start school in January.

There was always a pattern of normalcy in his life and ours, though the balance of how much was normal wore away over the next few years like ice melting in a water glass. He worked out most days, ate a full breakfast (even if it was noontime) (two eggs sunny, cottage cheese, peanut butter toast, a glass of water), snorted at the news when Bush & Co. appeared. He attended classes, got good grades, showed up for work on time and worked hard at his job. He made dinner for us some nights. Every Tuesday morning for one semester we found fresh danish and eclairs and lots of other really rich things we shouldn't eat on the counter from his Monday night pastry class at college. He gave us thoughtful gifts. That first Christmas home in 2007, a hummingbird feeder for Heather and a replica of a Remington statue for me, commemorating a daytrip he and I had taken in upstate New York that included a stop at the Frederic Remington Art Museum in Ogdensburg.

It's neither fair nor accurate to blame his alcoholism on the Army. His problems with booze and drugs went back through high school, and even delayed his enlistment by several months because he failed a drug test a week or so after he'd smoked some weed. For many like Francis, it was such problems that made the Army a salvation of last resort.

Nor on Francis.

A multi-generational strain of alcoholism had metastasized in his genes like kudzu weaving its way over every southern billboard and cypress tree it can latch onto. Another story for another time – of great uncles, great-great uncles (and probably great-great aunts, though I didn't hear about them as a kid), a couple of grandparents, and me. I'd been in remission for over twenty years when he joined the service, decades that would have vaporized with one drink. You're never not an addict if you are one. Just sometimes you find ways to manage it. And more than manage it, to live.

But now he had another eighty-pound backpack to slog

around, only we couldn't see it – his picture of Dorian Gray, his hurt locker.

Early one morning, just weeks before Heather's mother died and only a couple of months after he'd moved home, I went downstairs to the office, coffee in hand. There he was in the family room, passed out in an armchair, TV still on, empty scotch bottle on his lap.

I felt no anger at that moment, only deep distress and sadness, and alarm. But I also didn't want Heather to know. I shook him into groggy wakefulness and told him to stash the bottle and trot upstairs to his room before she saw him.

What would be gained by doing otherwise? Or bringing it up later with Heather as her mother was dying?

I gave him space, left him a scrap of dignity.

Avoided a scene.

Here's a rule: Don't argue about anything that matters with someone who's drunk.

Later, I quietly asked if he was all right and let it go with a nod. The moment slipped away. Life washed over us. Heather's mother died. My father was diagnosed with cancer. A Cooper's hawk appeared in the backyard two days in a row and left behind a feather that I wore in my hat.

Months passed.

And then Francis ran his car into a drainage ditch just a block from home. Car totaled. Towed away in the morning. He'd been drinking and passed out.

One way his addiction was different from mine was that he was farther along in self-awareness than I was at his age. He was candid about his struggles with it, willing to talk. I often had the feeling that he was just a breath away from putting it out of his life and finding some peace with himself, but he was stuck on that ledge looking down into the waves.

And he was dealing with some shit I never came close to with my student deferment in the early 1970s.

At dinner one night, he said that because he loved cooking so much people sometimes asked what's the best meal you ever ate. But he didn't like to say.

"What was it?" I asked.

He hesitated. "An MRE."

Funny thing, he said, is he didn't even remember what was in it.

Heather and I sat there wondering what he'd been through that day. Which he didn't tell us, though it's obvious he did remember that.

I sampled an MRE one time – not the best meal I ever ate.

By now we knew he was better off here than on his own. He wasn't here just to save money. He was afraid of being alone. But how much could we handle, and after a point, even help him?

We doubtless had a mollifying effect on him. Still, he drank almost daily and heavily. We lived in a state of continual stress because we never knew what to expect, especially in the morning, when we'd find him asleep in the family room, bottles stashed in the usual spot behind the sofa, as if that concealed them (as if even he thought it did – another soft cry for help). The heavy aroma of stale booze hung over the room and even swept upstairs to the hallway on such mornings and instantly sucked the newness out of the new day when I stepped out of the bedroom. "Helluva way to start the week," I noted bitterly, wearily in my journal one Monday a year or so after he'd come home – tip-toeing around, keeping voices down, stifling kitchen noise – the oppressive mood of helplessness, even entrapment.

The incidents grew worse. Before dawn on Christmas morning that year, I found him slumped over at his computer, partly dressed, pants off, bottles on the table. I sent him upstairs, where he collapsed into his bed. Many hours later, with a house full of people, including Alex's future in-laws, as he was in the kitchen talking to his grandfather on the phone in the usual holiday call hand-around, he suddenly turned toward me, seeking me out with his eyes in the chaos of cooking and guests and family and chatter that surrounded us. Shock waves of recognition rippled over his face as it came back to him. He'd blacked out and just now remembered. He handed the phone off as if it was a hot ember and darted up to his room. Later, weeping through his shame, told me he'd taken a double dose of Ambien *and* been drinking all night.

On another night he called and asked to talk to me. He was in a nearby shopping plaza sitting in the back of a squad car. The cop, it turned out, had also served in the 10th Mountain Division and wanted to cut him a break. He was cordial and professional with me, but told Francis sharply that there'd be no next time and he needed to get his shit together. I put my no-arguing-with-someone-who's-drunk rule into effect as we drove home. In the driveway, I said, "Just go straight upstairs and get some sleep. I'll talk to Mom."

Which I did. And did not argue with him, even the next day.

That may sound unremarkable, but we had some history between us from when he was younger. As a teenager, he was exponentially the middle child. So it wasn't unremarkable to me that I responded as calmly as I did to these incidents. In fact, I never did argue with him, and he never did with either Heather or me. But we were being eaten up inside – as much, too, because we could see that that's what was also happening to him.

Booze and drugs are symptoms. The malignancies run deep. Addiction a disease that he and many others brought with them into military service, too. And now he also carried the memories and guilt of all that his deployments had piled on.

Maybe we were lucky – he was lucky – for a while, anyway. He had a home to come to, parents and family who cared, stability. Many of the guys he served with came home to much worse – unfaithful wives, broken homes, poverty. One of his friends ended up divorced, in jail, and then committed to a psychiatric hospital after he returned. In Afghanistan he'd been awarded silver and bronze stars for valor. A time came when we told Francis he needed to move out. We were cracking under the strain. I could see it physically in Heather, an unnatural pallor, a pervading sense of dreariness, at times despair. She attended Al-Anon and Nar-Anon meetings, prayed, visited a therapist. Sometimes she'd simply go in a bathroom and weep. So did I.

"You can have as much time as you need to find a place," I said.

He was stunned. "I can't!" he sobbed. "I can't! I'll be dead in six months if I'm alone … don't … I can't!"

He didn't move out. That was about six months before we lost him.

Homeland

Every day and every minute were not like this. Rather it was more of an undertow, always there in the churning waves, always ready to snatch at our bicycling feet, sometimes pulling us under for a few panicky moments before we recovered, while at the surface we all lived on. When he was rested and sober and nourished, he amused us with his cynical wit. He admired Lebron James for staying out of the trash talk wars. He took his younger cousins fishing when they visited. He helped me wash windows and clean gutters, and kill a snake on the front porch one afternoon. He rode his mountain bike hard on local trails and came home bruised, regretting his stupidity and looking sheepish when I asked why his helmet was still hanging in the garage while he was gone. Didn't like wearing it, he said. Couldn't enjoy the ride. I didn't argue. Did this even register on the scale of his risk-o-meter? He cooked for us, and sometimes even cleaned up afterwards. He sneered at Rumsfeld and Bush on TV.

A waitress was crying upstairs in the kitchen.

Customers had been mean to her, she said.

Mean. Her word.

The cooks and servers didn't care about politics, global warming, the wars.

People didn't care about any of it.

They didn't know how they lived, how remotely, how ignorantly. Crying over a *mean* customer?!

"People don't know!"

I pictured him in the semi-darkness, the exposed stone foundation walls, the wine racks behind glass doors, the empty wood table tops, scarred and worn and always covered with freshly laundered white table cloths when guests ate down there in the stage-set brightness of good cheer and faux-newness and general upscale, solid portfolio, heavy insurance, heavily mortgaged house, and leased Lexus satisfaction. Overhead, the rumble of footsteps, clatter of dishes, echoes of kitchen noise in the stairwell. Him sitting on the edge of a chair, bent over, leaning into his phone. Sobbing.

He'd had two DUIs by now. Was driving with a suspended license – allowed only for work and school, but he blew that off and went wherever he wanted to go.

Just a few weeks earlier, the U.S. had pulled out of the Korengal Valley after five years of building outposts and bombing the shit out of the place. Back page story, quietly announced in a low-key press release. Five years of fighting and killing and hardship for nothing. No gains by anyone. Much lost. Afghan lives, American lives.

I knew he knew this and it bothered him. It wasn't at the center of this moment, but the world he occupied was so much larger – and uglier and deadlier and more corrosive – than the one at the top of the stairwell that he couldn't squeeze himself into that one. A world in which a waitress cries over a mean customer and no one cares about much of anything beyond the next meal, served or eaten. So it felt. So it was for him.

"The pain doesn't fade – it's more like energy that just transforms itself – from heat to gas to flames, from heat & cold into storms – always moiling into new shapes. It becomes resident, takes up space within, informs all interactions. This is its nature. It has submerged & embedded itself from the pronounced thing it was to become part of me, and will always be so."
—Journal, March 20, 2013

Rust on the Hillsides

> 'O hell!'
> He thought – 'there's things in war one dare not tell
> Poor father sitting safe at home, who reads
> Of dying heroes and their deathless deeds.'
> —Siegfried Sassoon

AT THE HEIGHT OF summer, driving Trail Ridge Road in Rocky Mountain National Park sometimes feels like caroming through an Edward Abbey nightmare – caravans of traffic, tailgaters, bikers rumbling through on tides of infrasonic waves that threaten to shake the needles out of pine trees. It's not uncommon to see people zoom up to a scenic overlook, jump out of an idling, window-tinted SUV, snap a photo, and then reseal themselves in the air-conditioning while the kids in back watch a video and Grandma enjoys a glimpse of the snow-capped mountains before her window abruptly hisses shut and they zoom away. People do this and worse in our national parks. David Brower, the Sierra Club's first Executive Director, wanted the roads in national parks to remain unpaved. You had to earn the backwoods, he believed. You shouldn't be able to drive there just like that.

But they are paved, and the national parks are still a great thing, and over many years of bringing our children here, we learned to skirt the Abbey nightmare. They didn't always love it, but as they grew our children (to our amazement) thanked us for the times we roused them before dawn to take in an awesome sunrise from above the timberline or head out on a trail while the dew was fresh and we could see wildlife that hid itself later in the day from chattering crowds tromping through in noisy clumps and wondering where moose and mule deer and ptarmigans kept themselves.

Francis and I came here for a week of camping in late September 2007. The caravans were gone and the place seemed to breathe with relief that its work was done for the season, like the hour after the last guests disappear into the cold night on Thanksgiving. Trail Ridge Road would soon close for the season because snowfall makes passage at higher elevations impossible. We arrived on a weekday. School was in session and vacation season over. It was almost startling to find the road so quiet and easy and lonely. We hadn't passed another vehicle or seen another human for miles. We'd both fallen into the silence of wonder. The evening was clear and windless. A veil of mist rose up from the meadows and wove among thickets of lodgepole and ponderosa pines. Quiet itself is a casualty of our time. Even when it's an option, we find it so, well, disquieting that we fill it with music and talk and the distraction of our smart phones, as if quiet were a vacuum, an emptiness. We fail to recognize its presence. Human sound is ubiquitous. Beneath the strata of incessant earbud music and TV babble are layers of traffic and air conditioners and construction machinery and airplanes and lawn mowers and the noxious howl of leaf blowers. The mountain vistas get all the attention here while quiet is an underappreciated attraction. You can't photograph quiet.

We arrived at Timber Creek Campground on the west side of the park at 6:15 p.m., with enough daylight remaining to set up camp and fix dinner. Twelve hours almost to the minute since we left home. A bonus day of sorts since we'd planned to camp one night along the way but then changed our minds and drove on, taking the western route to the park through Berthoud Pass and Granby and Grand Lake. Even in season this area of the park is generally less trafficked. On this day it felt pristine. We'd just zoomed across Kansas and eastern Colorado in a day, a distance that would have meant months of hardship and jeopardy just a hundred-and-fifty years ago in a prairie schooner. Where an ocean of bluestem and Indian and switch grasses that can grow to nine feet or more once swelled in the current of southern winds, from Interstate 70 we glimpsed the World's Largest Prairie Dog, a crude plaster statue that peeks over a fence at a tourist trap where you can also see two-headed sheep and other oddities of nature surrounded by cornfields and oil derricks. We stopped for lunch near Russell, Kansas, hometown of Senator and one-time Presidential candidate Bob Dole. A display of oil-drilling equipment at a sales outlet graces the roadside there. Russell was featured in a TV ad years ago in which local merchants pretended Senator Dole needed identification if he wanted to use a credit card. Our sense of arrival at Timber Creek might have seemed disproportionate to the relatively easy, if tiring, drive, but we suddenly felt like we'd entered another world.

At the unmanned campground office, we registered the Jeep and bought firewood on the honor system by filling out a form, folding it into an envelope with some money, and slipping it into a metal tube. We had our pick of sites and settled at the edge of a marshy meadow where elk gathered at dusk and remained throughout the night.

My brother Chris has a term for this kind of camping – famping, he calls it, as in family camping. Car camping, some say. I snorted smugly the first time I heard it. Not real camping, we agreed, Chris and I, as in tussling packs crammed with North Face-Columbia-Kelty-REI-Campmor gear over miles of backcountry trails, sweating into our sweat-wicking clothes in raw, high-altitude sunlight, and zipping ourselves into our insulated mummy bags on cold nights. To us, that was the real thing.

Now, out here with Francis, my brother and I seemed like kids in a backyard tent. Francis had slogged a heavy backpack and a lot more over miles of goat trails and bouldered his way across rocky and steep mountainsides, where well-trained, well-equipped men wanted to kill him and everyone with him. Twenty-four years old and he'd already fought in two wars. First a year in Iraq, and now just a few months removed from a sixteen-month tour in Afghanistan, with the Army still looming in his rearview mirror like a gleaming Peterbilt radiator grill bearing down on the interstate. We'd talked about this trip for months. No long treks. No big packs. Find a quiet place to camp, take some day hikes, sit by the fire in the evening. Famp.

Our campsite is sheltered in a stand of mature pines. To the east, the forest rises up into hills whose crests are hidden in the density of trees. The marsh to the west is fed by runoff from the Colorado River, which snakes and curls through the woods beyond our sightline. The Colorado is a wide creek here, hardly the legendary river that roars through Grand Canyon. Its headwaters are only a dozen or so miles to the north, fed by snowpacks at higher elevations. We'll hike up that way in a couple of days. We're also enclosed on the west, beyond the river, by a hillside thick with ponderosa and aspen, both of which favor the warmer exposure they get there. Driving up we'd been startled by the low water level at Grand Lake, where boat docks rested limply on the cracked and barren lake bed. Pine beetle damage has also ravaged the forest – trees dead and dying from infestation, swaths of hillside looking as if they'd been graffitied with Rustoleum by some giant ogre.

The sun has fallen behind the ridgeline, leaving a faint gray glow and rippling streaks of pink on the underbellies of clouds. From our campsite, in the dim light that remains, we notice more rust on the hillsides. This destruction is new to Francis, and unexpected. He'd asked what caused it as we drove by the lake, and I described how the pine beetles thrive in warmer temperatures and that recent winters haven't been cold enough to kill them off. One fact led to another, not my intention to travel this path, but there it is: drought, disappearing snowpacks, receding glaciers – all symptoms of a warming planet, the fever of breathing the toxins we've exhaled from billions of tailpipes and smokestacks and from mowing down the planet's lungs in rainforests to the south and boreal forests to the north in our fevered jones for more of the black drugs we mainline and whose waste we've deluded ourselves into believing simply dissolves benignly in the heavens. The worst thing about pine beetle rust is this: it's unstoppable. Ultimately it will claim everything as it spreads through the mountains and across the forests. But the truth, the facts, history itself felt too sullen to share. I stopped short of rambling my way back to the Industrial Revolution. Besides, he'd seen plenty for himself on both tours – polluted rivers, oil spills, sewage, trash fires, abandoned and burned out wreckage, well-head flames sending plumes of black smoke into the sky, many-tonned armored vehicles idling and rumbling everywhere at four miles to the gallon. War is the ultimate environmental disaster.

At home when he observed Heather and me saving banana peels and coffee grounds for our compost bin, he impishly described the stench of bonfires fueled by human waste. Bailing out the Titanic with teacups, we were.

"You think it's bad here," he said on leave one time. "You should see it there. Nobody gives a shit."

But the years of coming here and other places like it hadn't been wasted. As much as he'd resisted the daybreak hikes when he was a kid, the fact that he wanted to come here now spoke for itself. In recent years, too, he'd complain to me about his conservative Army friends who thought climate change was a hoax. Their resistance to facts, to actual information, while they recited the memes of Rush Limbaugh and Bill O'Reilly and Fox News, where every hour of every day doubt was strewn, falsities proclaimed, ad hominem attacks on Al Gore and advocates for environmental sanity prevailed, would agitate him into fits of frustration. He'd come to me for new facts to bolster his arguments. I was pretty sure his buddies were simply baiting him. He never got that nothing would convince them when they could always resort to claiming that the "facts" had been doctored or scientists had a political agenda or were greedy parasites who thrived on government grants (noted without irony and blithe indifference to the mega-salaries of oil executives) or that there was dissent in the scientific community, even if that "dissent" amounted a few white papers published by "think tanks" like the Heartland Institute and underwritten by the Koch Brothers and ExxonMobil. Not that any of them were reading these white papers. In fact, his friends were typical of the generally more conservative stripe of soldiers who enlisted to fight in these wars – volunteers who believed George W. Bush was a great leader, that Americans were engaged in a righteous cause, that down deep, this was a crusade, not a war, and the western values of Christianity and the free market (somewhat jumbled together in their thinking, as it was and is in the broad universe of conservatism that has smothered fact-based discourse on an epic scale in American culture) were the divine right of western civilization. But it was also true that the nature of their mission – and the chameleon-like vagueness of the policies that drove it – reinforced this type of thinking during deployments, especially in isolated and hostile places. As Paul Fussell points out in his book on World War I, *The Great War and Modern Memory*, "Since war takes place outdoors and always within nature, its symbolic status is that of the ultimate antipastoral."[1] Nature was not a friendly place to soldiers stuck in under-supplied outposts for months at a time in Eastern Afghanistan's mountains. It was easy to dismiss global warming as they froze their asses off and worried more about enemy gun positions and caches and having air-dropped supplies stolen by local villagers than about science or politics. It was also a testament to their love that their disputes about climate change strengthened rather than frayed their bonds of friendship with Francis – and a testament to my son's strength of character and intelligence that he was willing to be the lone voice of reason despite the peer pressure to cave into the Fox News chorus and ditto whatever Rush Limbaugh said on Armed Forces Radio, where he had a ready and attentive market every day on military bases throughout the world.

Francis's Army friends only knew him as *Frank* or *Sommer*, or by the Afghanistan deployment, *Sarnt Sommer*. His friend Isaac's eyes brightened with glee when his given name came up at our gathering after the funeral. When they first learned that Francis was his real name, Isaac said, it was like the gates were thrown wide open for new ways to taunt him. Unknown to his squad, Francis's name had been a lifelong source of torment as he grew up in the Midwest, where it's less common. It's my middle name, and also my uncle's, and was also shared by a

---

[1] Paul Fussell, *The Great War and Modern Memory* (Oxford U.P.: 1975, 2000), p. 231.

couple of other distant relatives on both sides of our family. In New York State, where Heather and I grew up, it's a common name, especially in Irish Catholic families, like mine. But here in the Midwest, it's a girl's name – and always misspelled *Frances* – as he was reminded by every teacher and adult and kid who heard it for the first time, or so it felt to him, as such things do for a child. So now the soldiers knew his name and it was open season on *Francis* once again. But his eulogist, Matt McKenzie, turned all that around when he chose to describe Francis by looking into the etymology of his name: "*Francis* is of French origin," Matt said from the pulpit, "and means free man. Even in the Army, when you aren't a free man, he was! He always did what was asked of him and always led from the front, but ... his views were not those of a typical soldier, which made him freer than most." This was code. Matt was among the most obstinate of the climate change deniers Francis butted heads with – as well as on a potpourri of other social and political issues – yet Matt also drove for fourteen hours, in uniform, after a full shift on duty at his post in San Antonio, to arrive in time for Francis's wake.

As our eyes adjust to the gray dusk, we notice elk in the marsh – a cow, a bull with a labyrinthine rack, ten, maybe twelve points, that seemed to float over his head. Others soon appear in the mist. The startling thing is realizing they've been there all along, their coats and colors and even their subtle movements fused into the shadows and hues of the meadow. It is an epiphany that repeats itself in the coming days and nights, the sudden flutter of trout in a stream, the vastness of constellations that are swallowed into the sodium-lit glow of our suburban nights at home. The elk snort and chew on marsh grass, their footsteps deliberate in the mucky ground. It is rutting season. Young bulls appear at the edge of herds or call from across the forest, eager to test themselves against older males for rights with the harem. They bugle in piercing, shrieky calls. We soon discover in these haunting echoes the counterpoint of challenge and response, the threat of a newcomer, the declaration of rights by the keeper of the herd. Dissonance shapes itself into syntax. What seems at first a chance sighting evolves into recognition – this world we're observing is organized, it has patterns; its society follows certain customs and mores. We are, we realize, visitors, interlopers – while for them, this *is* the world.

    Francis sleeps well that night, tightly wrapped in his bag, while I find myself restless. It is cold. The elk bellow in ghostly cries that echo like fire sirens in cavernous nighttime city streets. I might have slept through the noise, but we'd just arrived at an elevation of 8,900 feet, having started from the flatlands at about 1,000 feet that morning. I've had altitude sickness before. The symptoms are familiar. A promising night in the mountain air turns into an ordeal of headache and nausea. Francis is probably still acclimated from trekking through Afghan mountains. That plus years in the Army have conditioned him to sleep wherever and whenever he could because he never knew when he'd get another chance.

    Sometime before dawn, getting up, making a fire, and drinking coffee have more appeal than tossing in the sleeping bag. I wrap myself in a blanket and watch the stars and listen to the elk by firelight. It's difficult to imagine wanting anything more just then. The planet is a serene place. I toy with the notion that I can feel it moving through space, hovering in its radial course around the sun, dangling among galaxies and constellations. I recognize that the constellations aren't just overhead; they surround us, they're beneath my feet too. The fragility of our presence, our existence, is the epiphany of that moment. I doze for a spell, more restful than I'd been all night. In my inverted metabolism, coffee makes sleep easier.

A few hours later we're readying ourselves at the trailhead of the Onahu-Green Mountain Loop. The pack with our lunch and rain jackets is a joke to Francis. He says he'll carry everything.

The Onahu Creek Trail, one spur on the loop, is familiar. I hiked it solo with a full pack a couple of years earlier and camped just below the timberline, near 10,000 feet, where I had a close encounter with a bear that ended well for both parties (not that the bear had much to worry about). I'm eager to share a couple of landmarks with Francis. The rocky path follows the creek uphill, so for most of three miles we have running water alongside and open forest all around. We pass glades of wheatgrass and view alpine hills sprinkled with scree above the tree line in the distance. Francis is an easy trail companion. There's experience in his stride. He leads with unhurried but even steps. Behind him, I'm sucking air and don't want to show it. His situational awareness is so acute he'd probably notice a leaf fluttering at fifty yards if it seemed wrong for some reason, but he never says a word about my breathy effort to keep up with him. We don't talk much between breaks for water and scenery anyway. I've never understood how people can chatter their way along trails like this, how their gabbing is worth the price of missing out on all that surrounds them. Needless talk here seems intrusive. It is a place to feel small, unimportant, to become a receptor, to re-calibrate one's place in the natural cycles. Mankind is the only creature who contributes nothing to nature while plundering it for benefits that far exceed his needs.

We revisit my past campsite and the creekside where the bear thrashed about all night in the switch grass while I lay wrapped in my bag about thirty feet away. Paw prints were everywhere in the morning and grass matted all along the creekside. Now I regret not getting out of my tent and creeping through the darkness to see what he was up to. Courage didn't come so easily that night. We admire the meadow from the timberwood Onahu Bridge and take our lunch nearby.

On the far hillside, across a deep valley, the pine beetle rust has progressed since I was last here, even more so in the forest surrounding The Great Meadow, as it's known, farther along the trail. As broad and deep as its name, the meadow is a field of western wheatgrass, bluestem, and other grasses that form a natural ecotone between sub-alpine and alpine regions. In the distance, ponderosa pines spotted with rust blanket the slopes below the rocky scree of rolling hilltops. I take a photo of Francis in the field, which is now amber, almost golden, the color of wheat fields in Kansas. He wears camo BDU pants, a T-shirt, and his Kansas City Royals cap. He said the camo was better suited to this outing than anything else he had, and more comfortable. Also he didn't expect to see anyone he knew. He rarely wore Army clothes or paraded that part of his life. Never got a veteran's license plate or put stickers on his car. Detested yellow ribbon magnets and fat civilians parading about in American flag T-shirts silk-screened with post-9/11 war-whoops: *These colors don't run! Home of the free ... because of the brave! Freedom is not free!*

What do they know about it? he'd say.

The photo reveals how fit he was. There's a swagger in his stance, but none in his eyes. Usually he smiled easily for photos, even if he wasn't in the mood, but that day the blankness remained, a kind of disorientation which I only noticed weeks later when the film was processed. The thousand-yard stare. A cliché maybe, but also a misnomer. It's not the catatonic, I-have-no-idea-where-I-am-or-who-you-are look we often imagine it to be. It's not, as it sounds, literally staring off into the distance. In the photo he's looking right at me. If anything, there's clarity in it, truthfulness, a sense that the perspective of everything around him has been rearranged so that he understands reality differently. It's a kind of dark Zen, resonant with tragedy, untold, unspoken, such as you never imagine in the eyes of your own child. I noticed it again that evening, as we sat by the fire after supper.

We didn't learn for a couple of years yet, when it was formally diagnosed, that he'd come home with cognition problems, that a kid with an IQ of 140 would sometimes get basic vocabulary jumbled up as he was speaking. He'd lost half of his hearing in one ear and part in the other from rifle fire and mortar shells, and he suffered from tinnitus – a high-pitched, incessant whine in his ears, like a faulty bearing in an electric motor. One kidney was damaged from the rucksack banging on his back over miles and years of marching. His urine sometimes ran dark with blood. He had hip problems, too, from the weight of his pack and the equipment he carried, which could run to well over a hundred pounds. But the worst of it came in the form of nightmares and flashbacks that kept him from sleeping at home. He later told Heather and me that he missed sleeping in his plywood hooch at the outpost in Afghanistan. I think he may have slept well in the mountains with me because it felt familiar.

Many soldiers return with far worse injuries – loss of limbs, sight, horrific burns. His friend Shane returned from Iraq following an IED attack when shrapnel ripped through his torso. Some – many – didn't make it back at all. But what I was beginning then to learn during this first full month after he'd been discharged was simply this: that Francis, like thousands of others, was living with a palette of invisible wounds – both physical and moral – which have an insidiousness of their own and which invade their lives darkly because of the confusing contrast between the world of war from which they've just arrived and the world of no-war they've now entered, a world pre-occupied with celebrity scandals, political gaffes, eating contests, and Black Friday madness. A world of no-war and no-sacrifice. Less than one percent of Americans had any skin in these wars. Most of the rest seemed to be at the mall or posting selfies on Facebook or watching reality shows that had nothing to do with reality.

That evening, as we watched the fire fade and listened to the screechy and haunting bugling of elk in the marsh, we suddenly heard a lone calf bleating on the hillside opposite the meadow – a desperate outcry, laced with the terror of abandonment and isolation. A mountain cat might easily get to the calf before it found its way back to the herd. We began to distinguish the mother's call in the cacophony below. The night was moonless. Beyond our campfire the darkness felt intensely black in the seemingly infinite woods that surrounded us. The calf's bleating continued for hours. Such a simple problem to us and so unsolvable for them. The calf couldn't find its way and its mother couldn't leave the herd. I awoke before dawn and realized that the noise had ceased. However it ended, the drama was over. Elk now wandered through our camp and moose were feeding in the meadow. We would never know if the calf found its way back.

On the night before he was to return to Fort Drum ahead of the Afghanistan tour, Francis came into our bedroom and sat in the rocking chair, a creaky antique inherited from my grandfather, more ornamental than for sitting. It groaned under his sturdy frame. Heather and I had already changed and were turning down the bed. His eyes were vacant and moist. He began to weep.

This was January 2006. He'd been in the Army for over three years. Iraq was behind him. Following that had been a year of training for Afghanistan. Within a few weeks, his battalion would deploy. He was a battle-seasoned noncom, a sergeant, a team leader – and he was terrified.

"I don't want to die," he sobbed.

What do you say to that?

You can't lie. You can't tell him he'll be okay.

We were all confronted with the reality that tomorrow morning might be the last time we'd ever see him or he'd ever be here again. He might be going to his death on this tour.

When he was sent to Iraq in 2004, as casualties mounted and beheadings and other horrors made headlines, we had naïvely wished he'd been sent to Afghanistan instead. He killed men in Iraq and saw many others die, friend and enemy, civilians, women, children. But this tour would be worse. They were going to one of the most dangerous places on the planet, Afghanistan's eastern mountains, and they'd be looking for Taliban fighters, who were organized and trained and well-equipped, in terrain that they had known since birth and where they had countless advantages that Iraqi fighters did not.

On one of his leaves, he brought home a flash drive with a video file. He only shared it with me. It may even have been classified. We viewed it in my office with the door shut. He didn't want Heather to know anything about it. The clip was short, ten minutes or so. It was taken by Taliban fighters who'd killed a Special Operations soldier and still had the man's body, which they filmed themselves abusing, likely for propaganda. They rifle through his pockets and toss personal items aside like trash. They taunt the camera with a family photo. They handle their weapons as carelessly as yard tools, as they kick the body and scuff dirt on it. The wooded and rocky surroundings resemble trails we've hiked in Colorado. The video is a cautionary tale. Soldiers at remote outposts could be snatched while relieving themselves only ten or fifteen yards from their camps. Francis knew that if he was taken, we might never know what became of him. He knew there'd be firefights, sometimes at close range. He knew he could be captured, like the man in the video, or that he could die in many other ways – and he did come close several times. But despite the terror we'd seen when he broke down in our bedroom, he returned from Afghanistan a year-and-a-half later heavily decorated for his leadership and courage.

One of the mantras of the infantry is that no one gets left behind. On a hiking break in Colorado, we were talking about camping gear and the like, and I posed a question – what if one of us was hurt? Since we were never more than a few hours of jogging back down to a trailhead, I said the other should go for help.

His face went dark.

"No!" he said sharply. "Never leave anyone behind. No one gets left behind."

He wasn't in the park then – though even so, he was right.

What if a bear or mountain cat appeared?

What if the runner also got hurt?

What if Taliban fighters came over the ridge?

Heather shared one time her belief, or awful realization, that Francis's death in a car wreck, alone, four years after he returned home – and after drinking far too much to get behind the wheel – was because that code broke down here at home in the civilian world. She wondered if maybe, if he'd been with his Army friends that night, they wouldn't have let him drive. She didn't blame the people he was with, only regretted that leaving no one behind was a code that also got left behind, and it might have saved his life. Such a thought never took the form of a conviction; it was more of a doubt, a question. It does not nag at us, but it was a possibility, a road not taken in the history of our lives. The drinking is not a story for this moment, but it has a lot to do with invisible wounds and invisible wars.

—⚋—

We packed out before daybreak on Sunday morning. An amazing drive eastward through the mountains and into the rising sun on Trail Ridge Road. In the course of thirty-some miles we passed two, maybe three cars. In over fifteen years of coming here, we'd never had an experience like this. We spotted a buck and several cows on a hillside, silhouetted in the glow of the sunrise behind them. I stopped the Jeep in the middle of the road and shut off the engine – unthinkable any other time – and we got out and watched the elk graze serenely for a spell before driving on. We opened our windows and let the cold air rush through. Francis watched the ridges and tundra pass, perhaps thinking that one cluster of rocks or another might have made good cover for an enemy machine gun position. But he seemed peaceful enough now, perhaps also remembering as such thoughts passed, that none were there.

In the fall after we lost Francis, Heather and I revisited the park. Grief engulfed us like thick fog. The trip was a chance not to get away, but rather to immerse ourselves in our loss. Grief does not want distractions. It wants focus. We wanted no other stimulation here. We needed clean air and quiet; we needed not to speak unless we wished. It was autumn. I wanted to show her an aspen glade where Francis and I hiked and which would now be glowing in gold and amber tones, as it was then. Toward the end of our visit we drove by the campground where Francis and I pitched our tent. It was barren now, every tree gone. It resembled a county fairground parking lot. The pine beetle blight had taken over. The Park Service had no choice but to remove the trees. The marsh where we'd watched elk and moose gather was fully exposed, visible all the way from the road. It looked more like a swamp than the wetland meadow we camped beside. It's important to see such things. Memory is not altered by truth, only strengthened. We need to see the classified videos and the caskets arriving home. Like seeing rust on the hillsides, and dying glaciers, and wars.

Bread Crumbs and Hatchet Marks

ON ONE OF OUR infrequent and brief satellite calls from Iraq in 2004, Francis asked me to take the phone where Heather wouldn't hear us. I stepped out on the deck and slid the door shut. His voice was empty and flat. He told me there'd been a friendly-fire incident and he'd killed an Iraqi translator. He didn't know why the man was in the line of fire, but he knew instantly what he'd done as he watched him crumple to the ground through the rifle scope. He told me this and then let the sentences hang. I could hear residue of his teenage self in his voice. He was just twenty. Still spoke in monosyllables. *Yes, no, I guess.* But this wasn't teenage reticence; it was pain and isolation and fear. War was not supposed to be like this, to include such ambiguities, inflict such guilt. He'd seen war on TV, in the movies. They hadn't shown this.

It was one of those moments – like the night police officers came to our door and told me he was dead – in which nothing you say will change the reality of what you just heard. And whatever you do say is incidental to the fact, the reality, which is now planted before you like the monolith at the center of *2001: A Space Odyssey* – immobile, resisting interpretation, devoid of meaning. A fact, isolated, standing free like that, has no beginning or ending, no narrative, no message or theme or imagery, and there's no way to by-pass it. When the police officer told me he was gone, I didn't ask was he sure it was my son, could there be a mistake? I knew that what he told me was true, that these two men in uniforms and buckles and guns had not come to my door without knowing what they were about, that asking were they sure would only postpone recognition of what I now knew to be true. People do that: *Are you sure it's him? Could there be a mistake?* But I didn't. My knees buckled. I made it to the stairs to sit down, and all I could think of was the awful and tragic irony that Heather and I had imagined this moment a hundred times while he was deployed, with soldiers in Class A uniforms where the cops stood, but now, over two years after he'd come home, still, after all that, we'd lost him. It seemed so unfair, so utterly banal. I recall muttering, moaning even, "This is wrong! This is wrong!" But however it happened, at war or in a car wreck, the reality was the same. The monolith had been planted before us. He was gone.

Not knowing what to say on that call from Iraq, but that I needed to say something, I began to talk, just to talk, just so he'd hear a voice, my voice. That's what he needed most. I was as much confessor as parent. He needed expiation, forgiveness, comfort.

"Are you in trouble?"

"No."

"What happens now?"

"Nothing."

"Are you okay?"

"Yeah."

"Have you talked to anyone about it?"

"Yeah, they've already reviewed it. I've been cleared."

Not what I meant, but I didn't press.

Nothing more would come of it. Nothing happened now. That's what I heard in his voice – the wonder of that notion. He'd killed a man, a member of his own team. The man was dead and now nothing. The translator had taken this job at great risk to himself and his family only to be killed by the people who hired him. All of this weighed on my twenty-year-old son.

I sounded like someone else on the phone, offering platitudes, saying things I didn't fully believe myself, as I danced over all that ran through my head, questions, images of the firefight, of the man dying in my son's rifle scope.

"It's not your fault."

"I know."

"You were doing what you had to do."

"Yeah."

We both bought into the fiction of what we said, hollow as it sounded even as we spoke. We were talking about *his* fate, whether *he* was in trouble, whether *he* was okay, while somewhere not far from where he was calling a new widow and her fatherless children were grieving. There was the monolith – nothing we could say would alter their fate or change what he'd done.

All this in about five minutes, while I watched a few birds flutter in the walnut trees behind my fence.

We both knew – he knew – that everything wrong with that war was compressed into what had just happened and now what we said. We'd gone there wrongly, turned anger and self-pity into jingoism and nationalism; we'd fucked up on an epic scale and now weren't even talking about the war's victims.

I went inside and returned the phone to Heather for the few minutes he still had and kept this to myself for a long time. He'd ask me to carry some of the burden, not spread it around.

When does an event become a memory?

The incident was already in the past, but he was living it still, and now, in some remote way, so were we, Heather and I. She'd been affected by this tragedy even though she didn't know what happened. Nor did the widow in Iraq know that a middle-aged man in the American Midwest felt great sorrow for her – and regret and shame, and he was angry, too.

We were all changing – being changed by events as they were woven into the fabric of our lives. A new pattern was emerging, dark, Cimmerian. The yarn was coarse. It would chafe. We would not remember this time as others did. We would continue to live it.

In later years, after Francis was out of the Army and home, more such incidents trickled out, briefly told, like leakage – the Taliban fighter he killed in Afghanistan at close range, indoors, and whose *Qur'an* sat on a shelf in his room; the children whose bodies he collected after a school was bombed; carrying his friend's lifeless body up a mountainside following a helicopter crash.

He wanted us to understand his pain – why he couldn't sleep; that liquor wasn't really liquor but medicine – but he couldn't tell the stories himself, as if they'd been censored, as if a legion of demons had entrenched itself inside him, each one the avatar of an incident on his tours, and with one censor-demon in charge who redacted all of the stories until all that was left were sheets of paper with thick black stripes that he tossed into the fierce hot wind as Francis sadly looked on.

So Francis found another way. He would guide us into the dark places these demons inhabited, leave clues, breadcrumbs on the forest floor, hatchet marks on the trees.

A couple of movies might help us understand. He asked us see one and rented the other just for us to view. You should watch it, he told me, pointing to a DVD he'd left on the coffee table. The first was *The Hurt Locker,* the second *Waltz with Bashir.*

The DVD of *Waltz with Bashir* remained in the case unviewed. There was probably a late fee when he returned it. We felt guilty, some, for silently passing on the movie, but even without seeing it we knew it was more than we could handle. Our moods then were dark and sad, and also frustrated and angry at times. We'd been infected too. This is not something you often hear about PTSD – how contagious it is, how you get it by living with someone who suffers from it. We often felt as if we were adrift in heavy seas and thick fog; we might capsize at any moment. We couldn't see the shoals, but we heard the muffled and distant echoes of his demons.[1]

---

[1] Like many military families, we discovered on our own and more by intuition than by consciously realizing what was happening to us that PTSD is infectious. The insidiousness of the contagion is also part of its nature – fueled by a powerful sense of isolation and loneliness. I didn't come to understand this fully until much later, after we'd lost Francis. Yet it is widely felt and experienced. *Mother Jones* published a penetrating overview, entitled "Is PTSD Contagious?" with the provocative subheading, "It's rampant among returning vets—and now their spouses and kids are starting to show the same symptoms," by Mac McClelland in the January/February 2013 Issue. Web: http://www.motherjones.

He'd been living at home for about two years while he went to school and worked. He'd lapsed into heavy drinking, in a sad way too, often alone and late at night while he watched movies like *Waltz with Bashir.* Others did not see this side of his life – when the invisible wounds became visible. He functioned well at work and school. To see him during the day going about his business, interacting with friends and coworkers, you wouldn't know how tormented he was, how guilty and just plain sad. He went many rounds with the alcoholism – rehab, AA meetings, counseling, drug therapy – but he was being eaten up from inside. He came into my office one morning full of life, as cheerful as I'd seen him in months. Dry for ten days, he said. Not a drop. He felt great. That night he got drunk and later, now full of shame, said he'd gone out to celebrate staying sober. Not a hint of self-irony in his voice. Booze is a gateway drug to that kind of dissonance.

About a year after we lost him I ordered *Waltz with Bashir* from Netflix. Even then it went unviewed for a month or more. We didn't watch any movies rather than return it, but there it sat, a totem of loss, an emblem of unfinished conversations and unrelieved pain. So it was with a sense of ritual that we finally did sit down to watch the movie. We were stepping back into his world, fulfilling the request he'd made more than two years earlier.

---

com/politics/2013/01/ptsd-epidemic-military-vets-families/.

Heather and I were also interviewed for a news story on PTSD while Francis was still on active duty (already showing early signs that something was wrong while he was still at Fort Drum and months before he was deactivated), so we asked that our names not be used; see Lisa Chedekel, "Most Stress Cases Missed: Army Admits Disorder Is Under-reported," *Hartford Courant,* Aug. 6, 2007. Web: http://articles.courant.com/2007-08-06/news/0708060418_1_ptsd-stress-disorder-soldiers

Losing Francis

Waltz with Bashir is the autobiographical story of its director, Ari Folman, an Israeli army veteran who comes to realize he has no memory of serving during the 1982 invasion of Lebanon, though he knows he was there. Folman begins a quest to recover his past, visiting friends who served with him and a journalist who reported on the war. In a recurring dream, Folman and his friends watch from a beachfront on the Mediterranean as Beirut burns. Through their different stories we piece together a narrative of the invasion.

The film is unique in many ways, most notably that it is animated. Folman and all of the characters appear as avatars. The animation creates a bleak mood, an impression strongly reinforced by laconic dialogue and the sepia tones of visual imagery. The movie's understated rhythm glosses the immanent sense of tragedy buried in Folman's lost memories, which ultimately reveal his part in atrocities committed during the war. He'd been assigned to a detail that lit the night sky with flares over a Palestinian refugee camp as thugs from the Lebanese Christian Phalange entered the camp and ruthlessly murdered hundreds of refugees, including women and children and the elderly. The movie closes by dissolving into actual footage of the carnage, its aftermath, and the terrible grief and suffering of the Palestinians. This movie is still banned in Lebanon.

Another war, another country, another language – yet this story spoke to Francis, and he believed it spoke *for* him. It represented something he wanted us to know about what he'd experienced both in the Army and later. Its overarching theme is memory – Folman's odyssey into the undiscovered country of his past. For Francis, I suspect, the country was known, well mapped, and he wandered its terrain continually. His wasn't a problem of forgetting but of remembering. How do you measure the difference in magnitudes of guilt between killing one innocent or many? How many others were there besides the Iraqi translator? And too, at some point, perhaps while he was serving or perhaps later, the lines between enemy and friend, guilt and innocence blur. Why else would he keep the holy book of an enemy fighter he killed? His conviction about his own guilt was profound. We know this from snippets of nighttime conversations with Army friends overheard through thin walls and from references in his emails. His sense of guilt left him feeling isolated and alone, a feeling that was only reinforced by the challenges of navigating his way through a world in which these wars do not exist, even as they rage on.

Folman portrays this dizzying paradox in a sequence depicting a short leave he took during the Lebanon invasion. His avatar wanders city streets at home in Israel where people sit idly in cafés and go about their business as if there were no war. He seeks out an old girlfriend and, still dazed from the battlefield he'd left behind only the day before, finds himself in a nightclub full of young people throbbing to disco music. This contrast, this indifference was one Francis knew well — and so did Heather and I, as we maneuvered our way through the wars and deployments with him while the world around us shopped and amused itself with video games and sports, both real and fantasy, and shed maudlin tears as "God Bless America" displaced "Take Me Out to the Ball Game" at seventh-inning stretches throughout

The Homeland, as it was now known. TV told us about people who skipped Thanksgiving dinner to camp out at Wal-Mart for midnight sales. Herds would gather at storefronts and stomp and shriek and trample one another as they prepared for the coming of the Christ child with bargain-priced TVs and artificial trees and cheap Christmas lights made by Chinese political prisoners. It wasn't that America forgot the wars, but rather preferred them varnished in the imagery of football-field sized flags and crisp color guards and awesome flyovers.

Watching *Waltz with Bashir,* we found less that we were learning something new than recognizing what we'd already seen. He missed his cot in Afghanistan, he told us. Sleep was troubled here, in his own home, his own bed. He was afraid here. Early one morning, I had to go into his room to get his keys. My car was blocked in, but I didn't want to wake him because he'd worked late the previous night, so I slipped into his room with all the stealth and deliberation of Poe's madman-narrator in "The Tell-Tale Heart," soundlessly, slowly. He was sprawled across his bed, arms and legs akimbo, as if his joints had disengaged. Then suddenly he sprang upright, stiff and confused and intent. For a moment I thought he might attack me. His eyes were open wide and utterly blank.

"It's Dad," I whispered. "I just need your keys. I didn't want to wake you."

There was a pause while recognition set in. The fear and aggression in his eyes had not fully faded when he said, "It would not be possible for you to come in here without waking me."

He moved the car himself, and I never entered his room again without knocking and waiting for a response.

In some ancient cultures soldiers would participate in "desanctification" rituals on returning from war, rites of passage from the cause that justified the killing and bloodshed and which now restored them to the morality and codes of civilian life. War booty was sometimes shared with those at home as a way of absolving soldiers from any sense that their motives were self-serving. Such practices further gave war a communal context. In recent times, returning soldiers may suffer from the recognition that their experiences are not part of a larger narrative shared by others.[2] Certainly this was true for the Vietnam War, and now for many soldiers it is also true of the wars in Iraq and Afghanistan, as they are haunted by the realization that it was all for nothing. Even in battle, many are fighting simply to endure and survive until the tour ends. Francis would sometimes say, "They can't stop time," as he counted the days down. But they did mess with the physics of time through extended tours and policies like Stop-Loss, the back-door draft that kept soldiers in war zones beyond their active duty contracts. Such practices only contributed to the sense of betrayal many felt.

In our recent wars, platitudes like *Thank-you-for-your-service* have displaced the ancient rituals, condensing them into a few words, a handshake, a knowing look. But what does the speaker think he knows, and what do such word-gestures mean?

I was with Francis at the hardware store one day when a stranger in a USA T-shirt and beat-up camouflage ball cap with

---

[2] See Brad E. Kelle, "Postwar Rituals of Return and Reintegration," in Brad E. Kelle, Frank Ritchel Ames, and Jacob L. Wright, *Warfare, Ritual, and Symbol in Biblical and Modern Contexts: Ancient Israel and Its Literature* (Society of Biblical Literature, June 15, 2014), 205ff.

an American flag stepped into the checkout line behind us. I could see his expression morph from curiosity to recognition to a subtle nod of approval as he looked Francis over. The buzz cut and stiff posture and flat belly are easy clues in our militarized culture.

"You a soldier?" he asked.

When Francis nodded, the man stuck his hand out. "Thank you for your service," he said. Francis shook hands politely and said no problem. As we walked to the car, he said he hated it when people did that.

"I didn't do anything for him," he said, and a moment later added, "What does he know about it?"

Francis detested the spectacle of patriotism, getups such as this man wore, gratuitous flag-waving, the subtle flavor of defiance in the man's word-gesture, in whose deep layers the tropes of Rush Limbaugh and Bill O'Reilly and the right-wing chorus fermented in a quiet and desperate rage. What Francis saw and heard was a man in a mask and costume uttering a bumper-sticker cliché that – in his mind, at least – gave him a partnership stake in the wars, earned by displaying the flag on a dirty ball cap and carrying a red-white-and-blue chip on his shoulder in defense of a notion of freedom that had to do with oversized trucks, abundant and cheap gasoline, and racist indifference to the victims of American bombs in Afghanistan and Iraq.

Such moments reinforced the feeling that the people who most supported these wars were also those who least understood them – and usually had no personal share in them. They left Francis feeling confused and angry. For what did he deserve thanks? he wondered. He hadn't joined the Army for this character's benefit. He'd become a killer. He'd done things he was not proud of – and he'd enjoyed it at times. And that confused him too. There was hardship, but there were also thrills, heavy rushes. There were badass big-boy toys; there was camaraderie and now life-long friendships with men who'd been there too. There were bad decisions, confusing decisions, and good decisions at every level. There were incredibly courageous soldiers for whom he would have died and who would have died for him, also those who were cowardly and unreliable and stupid – and he probably would have died trying to save one of them, too, if that's what he'd had to do. He resented stupidity and cowardice because they endangered others. We heard about such men – and we also heard from others about his own courage. "He led from the front," we were told. The opposite of hearing such stories isn't criticism; it's the sting of silence or its first cousin, faint praise, and we did not hear these as his friends called and sent emails and traveled long distances to bury him.

While *Waltz with Bashir* is autobiographical, the other movie he wanted us to see, *The Hurt Locker*, is fiction, a curious contrast since the former is animated while the latter is not. Francis told us that *The Hurt Locker* was the only movie he'd seen that came close to portraying what it had been like in Iraq.

Despite numerous awards and widespread praise, *The Hurt Locker* has been criticized by some Iraq veterans for various inaccuracies, most notably the idea that a loose cannon like First Sergeant Will James is representative of soldiers who fought there. Regarding the film's nine Oscar nominations, Paul Rieckhoff, who founded the Iraq and Afghanistan Veterans of America, remarked on Facebook that that was "nine more Oscar nominations than it deserves. I don't know why critics love this silly, inaccurate film so much."[3] But to Francis, who'd spent over a year there – and to us, too – Will James is a fictional character and his reckless and impulsive behavior less representative of soldiers in Iraq than a symptom in the larger allegory of America's addiction to war – and in particular its enthusiasm for entering this one.

James, portrayed with great intensity by Jeremy Renner, is an Army demolition specialist. He is unpredictable, impulsive, and obsessed in ways that compare with Ahab's monomania. His job is to defuse bombs and IEDs planted in urban settings where civilians are as much, if not more, at risk as American soldiers. His seemingly nerveless exploits often cross the line into recklessness, endangering his squad while winning accolades from his hyper-enthusiastic commander. He is, without doubt, exactly the kind of soldier Francis did not want to be around when things got hot. James becomes an emblem of U.S. recklessness, and we subsequently follow his inward deterioration as the war slogs on, as it did and still does for a "war-weary" public, as TV now describes us (mostly tired of hearing about it rather than tired of war itself, which has affected few Americans directly), and as

---

3 Christian Davenport, "Some Iraq, Afghanistan war veterans criticize movie 'Hurt Locker' as inaccurate," *Washington Post*, Feb. 28, 2010. Web: http://www.washingtonpost.com/wp-dyn/content/article/2010/02/25/AR2010022506161.html?sid=ST2010022603133.

It is not a small irony that the now-discredited (yet miraculously redeemed and re-employed) NBC anchor Brian Williams, who lied about his own experiences as a war correspondent "under fire," was among those to criticize the movie for a perceived lack of credibility, if perhaps only in order to boost his own unearned battle-zone cred.

his encounters with Iraqi civilians awaken him to the war's true consequences.

What Francis found most akin to his experience in Iraq was the in-country, on-the-ground atmosphere of the film – the hot, arid, crowded streets; the tensions of not knowing whom to trust; the fears, which Francis described to us, of wondering if a boy with his hand out for candy might have a knife or gun concealed in the other. (He told us to stop sending hard candy for the children for this very reason.) These tensions between the untrusting civilian population and the intrusive and violent military presence were only made worse as innocents were mistreated and killed, and individual soldiers with good intentions were also resented and attacked and killed. The invasion of Iraq had all of the ingredients for a disaster and that was what it became.

The film relies on two conceits, one set out in the movie's epigraph, which is taken from a passage in Chris Hedges' 2002 book, *War Is a Force That Gives Us Meaning:* "The rush of battle is a potent and often lethal addiction, for war is a drug." The sentence melts away on the screen as the movie begins, leaving only the words *war is a drug*. The second conceit resides in its title: a *hurt locker* is where you stash all of the pain, guilt, memories, and baggage – the soldiers' pictures of Dorian Gray, so to speak. Home to all the demons. While he's deployed, mainlining the drug of war, Will James leaves the locker shut and thinks little about its contents. But then he comes home and withdrawal sets in. Now it's just him and the locker's contents, the liberated demons, the bizarre contrast between all that surrounds him at home and the place he'd just been. He stands alone in the most ordinary of settings, a grocery store aisle, and stares in wonder at shelves filled with boxes and cans of food, all neatly lined up, not a vacant space on any shelf. The camera angle suggests a distant vanishing point and lends a sense of infinity to this abundance, while vacuous Muzak plays over the scene. Crowded places are anathema to many returning soldiers – certainly they were to Francis, who, on returning from Iraq, could not walk busy streets and stood immobile one afternoon at the doorway to a mall he could not bring himself to enter. In its understatement this quiet scene isolates what is perhaps most disturbing, a question with no answer that for many may not even find its way into words: how can there be *this* and also *that*? How can there be war there and me alone here on this polished linoleum floor with shelves full of food and mind-numbing music playing all around me? How can I have been *there* yesterday and *here* today? The wonder and blankness in James's eyes wordlessly crystallize that notion.

Like Ari Folman and Will James, Francis found himself in a world where the place from which he'd just come is mostly unknown. A new arrival from another planet, a stranger in a strange land. He carried within all that the images and latent experiences of where he'd been, reliving the awful dramas of the past while the world that surrounded him performed surreal burlesques on YouTube and Facebook and TV, in shopping malls, and in Washington. Returning soldiers like Francis discovered harshly that the so-called Homeland does not share their grief. How can it when it has mostly not shared in the war? He and waves of others found themselves in withdrawal from the adrenaline rush and camaraderie and the universe in which the hurt lockers remain locked. But once home, the lids blew open.

The drug of war is surely lethal, and even though it didn't kill Francis there, I have little doubt it killed him here.

The Art of Grief: 'Windows and Mirrors'

> *"Con mortuis in lingua mortua."*
> —Modeste Mussorgsky

BLOOD SEEPS THROUGH THE gauze on Salima's foot. It's what we notice first: the dark, rusty seepage a sharp contrast to the pastels of her pajamas and room. She's thirteen, we learn, but the distant look in her eyes belongs to someone much older. She sits squat on the bed, chin resting on her knee. She seems mindless of her burns. Her mother and sister also survived, but three others in her family were killed when the American helicopter opened fire on their tent in Kandahar

A few paces on, a boy stares at us wide-eyed. Americans in jeans, in coats and scarves, a funny wide-brimmed hat. What might he imagine of us and the distant and wealthy place from which we come? Maybe we have candy. His eyes are wide and blue. He leans on a walker, struggling with his new prosthetic leg. Behind him, stacked like so many rakes and shovels in a Home Depot display rack, stand rows of prosthetic limbs. One renegade leg with a shoe on its foot dangles from the shelf as if about to walk out of the painting on its own.

Murals tend toward bluntness. Images are large, broadly depicted, thick with meaning. They may have subtleties, but they are rarely subtle. The nature of the medium – from the Latin word *murus*, wall – invites simplicity and directness. City streets and alleys, interiors and exteriors of buildings become canvas. This isn't art created in a studio and then set outdoors, like a bronze statue in a city park. The setting, the place it resides is integral to its nature and creation. The audience is not museum visitors, but passers-by, and those who live with it. Murals may be illegal, even offensive, and they are impossible to ignore. For better or worse, such artwork becomes an element in the life of a neighborhood, a landmark, a defining characteristic, a part of the community. One may choose to go to a museum. Or not. But a mural on the side of a building confronts the viewer; it demands a response.

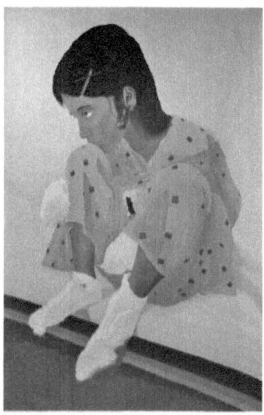

"Salima" by Nanna Tanier,
based on a photo by Paula Bronstein.

Losing Francis

Early twentieth-century muralists, from Northern Ireland to Spain to Mexico, all of which experienced vast political upheavals in those decades, are often credited with transforming this ancient art form into a socially- and politically-charged medium. They not only recognized the power of its visibility, but in regions where illiteracy was common, it was both an effective means of communication and also offered the oppressed a sense of unity. Mexico produced some of the most influential muralists of the twentieth century. Known as *Los Tres Grandes,* José Clemente Orozco, Diego Rivera, and David Alfaro Siqueiros[1] were political activists and artists. Their work spoke for the poor, the oppressed; for revolutionaries and peasants. Art with a social purpose, art for those who could not go to museums and for whom museum art did not speak. These muralists rejected the notion that art is the provenance of wealth and privilege.

Such is the context for *Windows and Mirrors: Reflections on the War in Afghanistan*, an exhibit of mural-styled paintings that toured the United States and Canada in 2011-12. Sponsored by the American Friends Service Committee (AFSC), a Quaker organization, this exhibit gathered works by forty-five artists, as well as drawings by school children from around the world, into what the catalogue describes as "a traveling memorial to Afghan civilians who have died in the war." Stylistically, these paintings offer a vibrant connection to the mural tradition: painted (or assembled, for several are collages) in broad strokes with graffiti-like imag-

---

[1] Rita Pomade, "Mexican muralists: the big three - Orozco, Rivera, Siqueiros," MexConnect website: http://www.mexconnect.com/articles/1064-mexican-muralists-the-big-three-orozco-rivera-siqueiros.

ery and highly accessible in meaning, symbol, and representation. Muralist John Pitman Weber, whose painting, *Learning to Walk Again,* I referenced above, is a co-founder of the Chicago Public Art Group and one of the project's organizers. The mural tradition, Weber said in a *New York Times* interview, had become increasingly "domesticated and institutionalized." He wanted *Windows and Mirrors* to be unapologetically political in giving voice to the civilian victims of America's longest war.[2]

"Learning to Walk Again" by John Pitman Weber.

And its most invisible. In late 2011, when Heather and I toured this exhibit at the Kansas City Public Library, it had been ten years since the invasion of Afghanistan, which began as the hunt for Osama bin Laden and then slogged through as many reasons for waging war there, it often seemed, as seasons that passed in all those years. In an untitled panel, artist Jessica

---

2 Kari Lydersen, "Afghanistan," *New York Times*, July 1, 2011. Web: http://www.nytimes.com/2011/07/01/us/01cncmurals.html

Munguia gathered the war's evolving mission statements into a collage of weaponry and military-speak, alongside images of an Afghan woman and child weeping. There has been no *Life Magazine* moment for this war, as there was over forty years earlier, when a black-and-white photo of a terrified, naked child running from the horror of napalm became the emblem of America's war in Southeast Asia. And unlike the invasion of Iraq, which by 2005/6/7 many Americans had begun to realize was both a mistake and a disaster, Afghanistan was still, ten years later, as we stood before these panels, regarded by many as a "just war" and its civilian victims little more than regrettable and faceless casualties, "collateral damage" (also the title of a painting in the exhibit) in the virtuous cause of "keeping America safe" – the go-to meme of American politicos who values their jobs and government healthcare.

Kansas City's empty downtown streets echo with our footfalls in the grey barrenness of a cold Sunday afternoon that we find oddly welcoming. Busy sidewalks and bright sunlight wouldn't have felt right. We are still new to grief. We'd lost Francis just ten months earlier. His Afghanistan deployment in 2006-7 had awakened us to this war's true victims. In the cavernous quiet of the Kansas City Library, where the display of *Windows and Mirrors* meanders through a gallery and adjacent hallways, we find a connection both to them and to him. These paintings complement our inner turmoil in ways that are at once soothing and enlivening. Grief is not something the grieving wish to abandon or suppress. Just the opposite – it rather seeks to be fully experienced until it's ready to cohabitate with other moods and sensibilities. Navigating even the simplest markers of life – meals, a trip to the grocery store, the changing seasons, a birthday – often feels like walking a cliffside path in thick fog. Unseen objects provoke spasms of fear and sorrow and tears. We grapple with the nagging sense that our son's death is an event, a happening, a circumstance we just need to "figure out," as Heather puts it, as if we can negotiate or reason with it; as if, like many problems parents face, once understood, we can fix it.

As the title suggests, *Windows and Mirrors* is at once a gallery of windows into an Afghanistan few Americans, including us, will ever see and a hall of mirrors reflecting who we are in the bitter reality of our presence there. For the artist, Theodor W. Adorno has noted, the "unsolved antagonisms of reality return in artwork as immanent problems of form."[3] *Windows and Mirrors* resolves – or synthesizes – these antagonisms in the conceit of murals now rendered on stretched parachute cloth (itself a suggestive medium in the context of this war) with identical dimensions, four feet wide by six feet in height, and hung museum-like in a way that would seem contrary to the mural tradition from which they're derived. This uniformity, also a kind of contradiction, further synthesizes the conceit, as the exhibit hints at allegorical settings that might range from the symmetrical fenestration of the Windows on the World restaurant in the North Tower at the World Trade Center,

---

3 Theodor W. Adorno, *Aesthetic Theory*, trans. Robert Hullot-Kentor (London & New York: Bloomsbury, 1997), p. 7.

overlooking the city and beyond, to a country church whose windows are populated by saints canonized through their own suffering. The gallery itself, through the uniformity of the panels' dimensions, becomes a many-windowed room that looks out on scenes of a war that terrorizes the most vulnerable of the Afghan people. The exhibit effectively becomes a single work of art, just as trees in an aspen grove are part of a single organism that spreads itself across a mountainside.

Heather and I find ourselves looking through these windows onto the world that changed our son – and us. These wars, Afghanistan and Iraq, and now Francis's death, have become crucibles for what matters and what doesn't. Our vision wasn't blurred by his troubles and now our grief, but sharpened. We'd long ago come to see American indifference to the wars not as passive neglect, but rather as a kind of depravity. Soon after the 9/11 attacks, President Bush urged Americans to go shopping. "Go to Disney World!" he exclaimed. Which mutated into a weird sort of civilian strategy to win the wars by pretending we weren't waging war. Patriotism Americans could embrace. War without pain. War without sacrifice. War without war. Just don't forget to "Support the Troops!"

―᛫―

We drift among the paintings. Our moods modulate through variations on sorrow, empathy, simmering anger. Across town, eighty thousand people have packed themselves into Arrowhead Stadium for a Kansas City Chiefs football game that afternoon,

The Art of Grief: 'Windows and Mirrors'

but even as we regret that more visitors aren't here, we're grateful to have the gallery mostly to ourselves. I wander off one way, Heather the other.

The sound of tambourines and drums, a wedding party gathering, laughing, singing now seems to rise up from *The 'Peace' Operations of the U.S.: Airstrikes on Weddings*, by Art Hazelwood and Juan Fuentes. In the distance, turbulent clouds billow where bombs have struck and will soon rain down on this gathering too. As symmetrical and infinite as a wallpaper pattern, a matrix of drone aircraft fills the sky overhead. The image references a well-known poster from the Spanish Civil War protesting the infamous bombing of Guernica in 1937, when German planes targeted a village of no military value in an act of sheer terror directed at civilians. According to the caption for *Airstrikes*, from 2001 through 2008, some 380 wedding celebrants were killed in Afghanistan in American bombings

"The 'Peace' Operations of the U.S.: Airstrikes on Weddings"
by Art Hazelwood and Juan Fuentes.

Losing Francis

Stories of more civilian victims are told in a series of textual panels. In one, laser-guided "precision" bombs destroyed a village in Eastern Afghanistan, and then, soon afterwards, as survivors clawed through the rubble in search of loved ones, hit the village again. The text cites a report from *The Guardian* in which a U.S. Central Command spokesman in Tampa, Florida, some 8,000 miles away, claimed "there was no collateral damage." But *Guardian* correspondent Rory Carroll walked the bomb site in Qalaye Niazi and reported seeing "bloodied children's shoes and skirts, bloodied school books, the scalp of a woman with braided grey hair, butter toffees in red wrappers, wedding decorations."[4] In another bombing, five women, three children, and an old man died in their hut when a 2,000-pound bomb hit their village. Elsewhere, a deaf man didn't know soldiers were shouting as he ran from them, so he was shot. Another man was killed while driving – too fast to suit American soldiers – to the hospital in search of his sister, who'd been injured in an attack. Over 3,700 Afghan civilians died in the first wave of American bombings in the fall of 2001, many more than were lost in the U.S. on 9/11.

The remoteness of these numbers – of the deaths of these civilians – is the central theme of *Windows and Mirrors*, which sharply rebukes American *civilians* for complicity in the tragedies depicted here. Invisibility provides cover for the war in

---

4 Rory Carroll, "Bloody evidence of US blunder," *The Guardian*, Jan. 6, 2002. Web: https://www.theguardian.com/world/2002/jan/07/afghanistan.rorycarroll. See also: https://ratical.org/ratville/CAH/civiDeaths.html; https://www.theguardian.com/world/2003/feb/13/afghanistan.rorymccarthy; http://www.tomdispatch.com/post/174954/engelhardt_the_wedding_crashers.

Afghanistan, even more so than for Iraq, where casualty counts and news reports ultimately – and tragically too late – led many Americans to question the purpose and ever-morphing rationales for fighting there: WMD? (nope); the "Global War on Terror"? (nope); al Qaeda? (nope); our "freedoms"? American freedom, as Andrew J. Bacevich notes, has in recent decades had more to do with abundance and unlimited consumption than liberty.[5] To sacrifice is to admit defeat.

Rikki Asher's *Bamiyan Buddha and Weeping Women* is a meditation on the strains of superstition and willful ignorance that brought down the massive statue of Buddha once carved into an Afghan mountainside, where it stood for centuries like an upright mummy in a sarcophagus. Over a thousand years ago, monks began journeying here on pilgrimage. Prayers were chanted through the Buddha's hollowed stone nostrils. But the nineteenth-century Afghan emir, King Abdurrahman, found the statue offensive. Its features seemed too Mongolian, too much like those of invaders who'd once overrun his country. So he ordered the face removed, leaving only a massive blank stone slab atop the statue. Perhaps, though, as the story was told and retold, it only served to remind new pilgrims of the statue's lineage. Perhaps they saw a trace of the Buddha's smile lingering in the spirit of the stone.

But the Taliban found even what remained of the Buddha objectionable. So in 2001 they blew the statue to rubble. No slouches when they undertook such a task, they hired demolition experts from across the Middle East and forced locals to dig holes for the charges, sometimes with bare hands. The explosions went

---

5 Andrew J. Bacevich, *The Limits of Power: The End of American Exceptionalism* (New Yok: Henry Holt & Co., 2008), p. 62.

on for days. Taliban radio traffic was lively with good cheer as the statue crumbled. Asher's painting anticipates its final destruction. In the foreground a woman wails, her pain almost audible, her image replicated as if in a series of mirrors receding endlessly into the distance, suggesting infinite grief as bombs fall from above – emblems of the unending war. Colorful icons frame the panel, based on regional textile designs. The artist describes their significance in a caption: 108 rectangles border the painting as a tribute to the Buddha: *one* representing *Bindu* (Creation), *zero* for *Shunyata* (Emptiness), *eight* for *Ananta* (Infinity). Each rectangle depicts a leaf of the Bodhi tree, under whose boughs Buddha gained enlightenment. Idea and image fused, human suffering and cultural ignorance grafted. A feeling thought, a thought felt.

Heather and I hook up again in a corner of the gallery, where she's landed at the image of a child about the same age as children she teaches. Francis's Afghan tour inspired her to establish an international club at school so her children could learn about cultures around the world and break through the barriers of provincialism. Now, ten years later, her club is the school's most popular activity. After a moment, and with a sudden breath, I wordlessly share the recognition she'd already discovered in this painting, subtle enough until you're upon it: thin streams of blood form a veil before a child's grim face. We contemplate her image. We raised three of own who never saw or even imagined the world through such a scrim. Many of the panels depict children – riding bicycles, playing soccer on smoking ruins in the shadows of drone bombers.

The Art of Grief: 'Windows and Mirrors'

"Mountain Kites" by Ann Northrup

To say one has a favorite painting in such an exhibit may seem odd, but it's our nature to make such distinctions, even here. Heather's is Ann Northrup's *Mountain Kites,* perhaps the most serene and hopeful in the gallery. A joyful child with her kite in an open field – an idyllic vision filled with possibilities. In contrast to the other panels, it seduces rather than shocks. In the foreground of a florid mountain valley, a child bundled in parka and hood smiles and clutches her kite, ready to launch it into the wind. Close by, her father has already set one afloat. The scene's tensions are themselves at odds. One derives from a simple and pleasing action about to unfold. The girl smiles broadly as if we'd asked her to pose for a snapshot before she scampers away to release her kite. This scene might as easily be set in Colorado or Spain or China or anywhere children fly kites. But context matters, and here, surrounded by the tragedies of this war depicted in the nearby panels, we're compelled to imagine the prospect of bombs suddenly falling on this scene too, even as we perceive history's road not taken, or yet to be taken, or taken still, despite the war. The artist writes, "I wanted an image that people could identify with, a child that they could fall in love with and that they would want to cherish and protect."

Photo by Jon Demler, circa 2007.

This is Francis surrounded by Afghan children – all boys, but for one bearded man in the background. Girls would not be allowed to venture out among soldiers like this. Some of these boys worked at the outpost, cleaning and doing chores. This photo was probably taken in 2007. Francis had grown wary of children in Iraq, but he always had a weakness for them and said he liked some of these kids. They'd be in their twenties now. I keep this photo on my desk and sometimes wonder what became of them, whether they joined the Taliban or Afghan National Army, or even survived the war.

In most of these paintings we view Afghanistan as observers, but in Lillian Moats's *Collateral Damage*, we become aggressors as we peer through the crosshairs of a riflescope and watch mortar rounds explode. Plumes of smoke fill the background, while close up, like a TV picture-in-a-picture, a girl watches through a window, sitting perhaps as she was in the moment before the bombs struck. Western eyes cannot avoid associating her sky-blue robe and white headscarf with traditional images of the Virgin Mother as she appears in church windows and on Hallmark Christmas cards. (Yet we don't ask ourselves how a young Middle Eastern woman of two millennia ago came to have the Caucasian features and the clear, pink skin of a cover girl.) But whomever this emblematic girl in *Collateral Damage* resembles, or doesn't, she is already dead by the time we see her in this painting. The white glow that fills her window will consume her in the next moment.

"Collateral Damage," oil painting by Lillian Moats.

I have suggested until now that we, Heather and I, looked through these paintings as if they were windows with a view of the Afghanistan war's victims, and that to the extent these images were mirrors, the reflections we saw, like Hawthorne's Hester Prynne spying the ominous figure of Chillingworth in the mirror behind her, were those of the culture that surrounds us. But what of us? What did we see of ourselves?

It is true that grief for the loss of a child knows no comparisons, that losing a child is as tragic for the wealthiest parent on the planet as it is for the poorest, but this is an unfair dodge. The people depicted here are victims of a kind of menace that bears no semblance to how my son died. In a large sense, we may all be victims of these wars, but the analogy breaks down when bombs start falling on your home. The child with his prosthetic leg in *Learning to Walk Again* would have seen in Heather and me unimaginable wealth and abundance, no matter the reality of our means, for whatever those means, we live in a more fortunate world than he. Our complicity is rooted in that world. We must acknowledge that Francis was part of the invading force and that we watched for news of him and his friends eagerly, while foreign casualties were also part of the background in such moments. Surely this is natural. And surely, too, just recognizing our complicity is not enough.

He died a civilian, a veteran, in early 2011, as the Fukushima nuclear disaster devastated the lives of more than a hundred thousand people in Japan and as the Arab Spring was unfolding across the Middle East. The climate of chaos from these and other events that year gave us near-daily reminders that as we grieved in our own way and time, sharing that grief with family and friends, and still sleeping (the little that we slept) in our own beds and eating (the little that we ate) as we needed, many others did not have

The Art of Grief: 'Windows and Mirrors'

such comforts as they faced tragedy. Our grief was blinding, stifling, breathtaking, but it had few distractions. Poet David Ray portrays a similar contrast of worlds in his sonnet "Bhopal," from *Sam's Book*, an extended elegy for his own son, who died at age eighteen in 1984, the same year that gas poisoning from Union Carbide's pesticide plant killed tens of thousands in Bhopal, India. The proximity of Ray's loss to that event – and distance from it – is depicted through the experience of Bhopal families who've not only lost their loved ones but even been deprived of the chance to mourn properly, with

> ... no time
> for weeping as when we lost our son Sam
> and stood, hands joined, to wish him well in some
> life beyond.[6]

They are, he adds, victims twice over because their brownness renders the deaths of their loved ones of lesser consequence in the First World, which is, of course, the source of their suffering:

> One thing that's certain though is this: Third World
> or one beyond, they're all our children now,
> though borne by millions in brown arms and black,
> and not much mourned by those who think their own
> are wonders, others somehow less.

---

6 David Ray, "Bhopal," *Sam's Book* (Middletown, Conn.: Wesleyan UP, 1987), p. 72. A recent example underscores the point: Following the May 22, 2017, terrorist bombing in Manchester, England, images and stories of the attack's 22 victims received exhaustive coverage, while less than two weeks later a massive bombing in Kabul, Afghanistan, that killed 90 people and injured over 450 was treated like a back-page story in most news outlets. See Amy Goodman and Denis Moynihan, "A Kabul Bomb Blast Has Killed at Least 90 People. We Need to Know Their Names," *Democracy Now!*, June 1, 2017. Web: https://www.democracynow.org/2017/6/1/kabul_bomb_blast_kills_at_least.

So there was complicity in our reflections, even if unintended. Was it fair to bring our grief here, to infuse the tragedies depicted in these panels with our own sorrow? This was more than a Sunday afternoon at the museum for us. More of a pilgrimage. Though, in retrospect, those gallery visitors who had no such loss to drive them here and still came, the few who did, may deserve more credit. Still, intent may not be enough. Privilege resides in a failure of recognition even more than the conditions of a life.

As of this writing, it has been six years since we experienced *Windows and Mirrors*. The website for the exhibit has since been removed. As we walked through the halls of the library that day, it was already evident that the war in Afghanistan would surpass Vietnam as America's longest war. It is now becoming America's endless war. According to a Brown University study, over 31,000 Afghan civilians have been killed since the American invasion in 2001, a number that, as stunning as it is, doesn't remotely approach the immeasurable devastation for hundreds of thousands of survivors of the violence there.[7] American losses in Afghanistan number over 2,200, with over 20,000 injured. President Barack Obama committed some 8,400 troops to remain in Afghanistan when he left office. His successor recently spoke of plans to add 5,000 more so America could "starting winning" again in Afghanistan, whatever that means.[8]

---

7 "Afghan Civilians," *Costs of War* (Watson Institute of International and Public Affairs). Web: http://watson.brown.edu/costsofwar/costs/human/civilians/afghan
8 Paul Szoldra, "What are we even doing in Afghanistan?" *Business Insider*, May 9, 2017. Web: http://www.businessinsider.com/president-trump-afghanistan-war-troop-surge-2017-5

The Art of Grief: 'Windows and Mirrors'

And still, the imagery from *Windows and Mirrors* remains with us in both imagination and fact. Heather displays a poster of *Mountain Kites* in her classroom. We keep pictures of two Afghan children from the exhibit on a shelf in our living room near a photo of Francis. If we came away with anything that day, it was finally the recognition that our son's death is one tragic speck in the vast tapestry of our wars, and that the victims, including Francis, are "all our children now."

Artworks in this essay appear by permission of the individual artists and with grateful acknowledgement to the American Friends Service Committee.

Further background on the exhibit may be found at these websites:

"Art vs. War – American Friends Service Committee's Windows and Mirrors." YouTube: https://www.youtube.com/watch?v=dQ7z0G65eCs.

"Deadly Embrace: The War in Afghanistan," *Afghanistan 101*, May 4, 2011. Web: afghanistan101.blogspot.com/2011/05/deadly-embrace-war-in-afghanistan.html.

Windows and Mirrors: The War in Afghanistan. Web: http://afsc.org/story/windows-and-mirrors-war-afghanistan.

"Sometimes I think it's like we each possess our own reality with Francis."
—*Heather*
*(my journal entry for Feb. 11, 2014,
the third anniversary of his passing)*

We Were Goats

Show me the two so closely bound
As we, by the wet bond of blood
    —Robert Graves, "Two Fusiliers"

"To be honest, sir, when I first met him I thought your son was a jerk."

We're standing, Bobby and I, in a restaurant parking lot in the French Quarter of New Orleans. It's a hot, humid August day, and I'm easing myself away from the idling pick-up's tailpipe and upwind of Bobby while he smokes.

I nod and grin. "Not the first time I've heard that."

In fact, I'm weirdly flattered, though I had thought I'd graduated from *sir* by then. Probably wanted to soften the remark. Still, his frankness puts me at ease.

Not much of a stretch to imagine Francis treating a new guy in his outfit roughly, and enjoying it too.

Losing Francis

—⚋—

On final approach a couple of hours earlier, as the plane slipped over warehouse rooftops, and car models became distinguishable on the highway below, I felt a surge of doubt as visceral as if the airplane, that close to the ground, had suddenly dipped in turbulence. Had I done the right thing coming here? Was I intruding? Bobby was probably waiting in the terminal. I wildly imagined him asking me outright why I'd come. Feet spread, arms folded, blocking the exit door. What're you doing here, sir? Calling me out for bringing my grief into his life.

Sir.

An hour later we were both weeping over half-eaten po' boys. It would be all right.

—⚋—

More than three years had passed since I'd asked him to give a eulogy for Francis. We spoke several times over the course of a day or two. The power of grief is staggering; it has all kinds of unexpected fallout. One is surely the way it thrusts you, in a matter of hours, a day, two days, into relationships that bond you with strangers, how new people come into your life with a presence as familiar as if you'd always known them. Suddenly names we'd only heard, and some we'd never heard, were in our living room and kitchen – soldiers and veterans, coworkers, school friends.

Francis often mentioned Bobby. As far as we knew, Bobby

Brandt was his closest friend in the Army. They served together in Afghanistan in 2006-7, Francis's second overseas tour and Bobby's first. He later redeployed to Afghanistan after Francis was out of the Army. Losing Frank, as Bobby knew him, was hard, but he was in school when it happened and had a young family. A plane ticket to Kansas City on short notice was too expensive. I knew he felt awful about not coming, so I called a few days after the services. He'd done more for Francis in life than he could do for him now, I said. That's what mattered. We promised to visit, here or there, a promise, I decided – I think we both did – that would not become one of those hyper-emotional impulses that fades into an itch and passes with time.

—ɯ—

Cindy Sheehan, who lost her son in Iraq, became the face of grief and anger for antiwar activists all over the country during the height of that war. Her sorrow led her to all the way to the front gates of President Bush's Texas ranch, where she camped for weeks. I understood this grief in new ways now. Her *self* had been displaced. Instincts took over. All there was was the cause she'd taken up – nothing she could gain would compensate for what she'd lost.

I, too, had become an actor in a play I didn't write. Grief has a way of distilling reality into its essence. While others may believe you're not thinking straight, that your perspective is distorted, in fact it's never been more focused, clearer, sharper. The world is anything but dark. Rather it is lit in the crystal glare of an arc light – what matters becomes obvious, while the flaws in all that doesn't are exposed. A friend told me I was radioactive. I didn't know. Radioactivity is invisible, silent, terrifying for others, but for me, not knowing I was radioactive, there was only the brilliance of an arc light revealing all that surrounded me.

I was taking the trip Francis never got to take, living moments he didn't have the chance to live. I wasn't there for myself but for him.

But I was there, and maybe hadn't thought well enough about how anxious Bobby and his wife Allison might be about having me stay with them for four days.

House guests, Ben Franklin observed, are like fish: they start to smell after three.

I'd reserved a motel room and rental car, but Bobby was having none of that. "No way you're staying anywhere else," he said. And oh yeah, cancel the car, too.

He is sturdy, solidly fit. Like Francis, I think, determined not to lose his Army body as time swells from months into years after his service. His beard is dense and evenly trimmed, and he always wears a ball cap, even in the house. (Before I departed four days later, I had to prompt him to remove it so I could get at least one photo without it.)

He waves from across the terminal and we meet, embrace. A nervous man hug. In the truck, he soon relieves me of my final-approach fears. He's talkative and open. He knows I'm writing about Francis. In fact, if there's a reason for me to be here, that's it – to fill the gaps in my story. Bobby is a link to the collective memory we've lost. "Ask me anything you want to know," he says. But I don't have a list of questions. I'm not here to ask how many men Francis killed in Afghanistan. The fighting was bad. I know some of the worst — and know that I don't know some too. The distinction between learning the truth and pulling at scabs becomes clear. It's not information I want — it's to know the people Francis knew, to sink myself into his life. My "book" becomes a fragile excuse for being here. I'm suddenly a passenger, not in the truck, but on this trip. I'll go wherever it takes me.

Which right now, since this is my first visit to New Orleans, is a driving tour of the French Quarter. Bobby is acting the good host. We pass storefronts and souvenir stalls along the Mississippi waterfront — the local version of every tourist town I've ever visited, the gimcrackery veneer of New Orleans for tourists, not pilgrims like me. My radioactive arc light exposes it — a stage setting, a myth. I decline the walking tour, and later at the kitchen table Bobby laughs as he tells Allison that when I said as much, he thought, "Yes!"

I feel triumphant. I've passed a test I didn't know I was taking.

Before the Army and before college, Bobby was a cook. He got his start making calzones and pizza in a local shop and then leveraged his experience into a job with a large restaurant chain, where he worked his way up to kitchen manager and later training manager. He traveled all over the country, and even to Kuwait, training chefs for the company's stores. But he didn't like the work. Big box restaurants are regimented; there's no creativity in the cooking; the kitchens are stressful and unpleasant. He decided to go to college and then law school.

The war in Iraq was raging then, as was the escalating U.S.

commitment to Afghanistan. During his junior year, Bobby, who Francis had long ago told me was archly conservative, got into a hot debate with an antiwar activist in one of his classes who argued that the wars were all about money and American imperialism.

So what was she doing about it? he wondered.

And then later asked himself, "Who am I to talk? What am I doing about it?"

That was the moment he decided to join the Army.

"If I can stop one fighter from killing an American, that'd be something," he said.

—⁂—

Bobby and Allison and their two children, Matthew and Elizabeth, live in a fishing camp on a canal that feeds nearby Lake Pontchartrain. When he first told me where they lived, I pictured the lakeside summer camp in New Hampshire I attended as a nine-year-old – cabins, a softball field, a beach at the edge of the lake. Anything but. Their house is on stilts, as required throughout the region following Hurricane Katrina. Across the highway is a state wildlife refuge. Behind the house, the canal drifts past, commingling fresh water from upstream with saltwater that comes in with the tide. There are two decks: from the lower one Bobby fishes for speckled trout and drops crab traps into the water. The glow of an underwater light attracts swarms of fish in the evening. Matthew fishes, too, and manages the traps expertly. Allison sometimes just shoots trout with an air rifle. Their freezer is packed with fish and venison. The upper deck overlooks marshland across the canal. From there each evening, I watched the sun set in dazzling colors and patterns that would have challenged even J.M.W. Turner to render. A steady breeze up from the lake offers relief from the heat. Over the next few days, I linger out here whenever there's down time.

At the house, literally under it, Allison skitters down the steps and clasps me instantly, almost tearfully. Six-year-old Matthew surprises me with a tight hug, as if I was an uncle he'd always known. To him, I'm "Mr. Bob," a Southern honorific I'd nearly forgotten from years ago, when Heather and I lived in North Carolina. He is bright and chatty and loves to play Mousetrap, which we play a lot over the next few days. Elizabeth, their six-month-old, "Little-bit," Bobby calls her, lets me walk her around the living room. My nerves return briefly. I take long, deep breaths for a few moments while I'm alone in the bathroom. We have several days ahead. Is just being here enough ... or too much? I'm determined to remain upbeat, play with the children; keep the focus off myself, my biases and politics, my grief. I'm not sure what I am now, what identity I have here. Who and what are the parents of a lost child to his friends? How do they fit us in? We want to belong ... but how? I'm not sure, but I'm here.

—∞—

Soon after we lost Francis, a soldier named Scott sent an email to us from Oklahoma. Like Bobby, he was fresh out of basic training when he joined Francis's company following its return from Iraq. "My first impression of him," Scott said, "was that he was a head-strong combat soldier just back and ready to make all the new guys' lives difficult."

Shades of the Bosnia campaign veterans who tormented Francis years earlier, I thought.

Scott's email continued, "Frank was one of the tougher combat vets to assist us new guys in our training, but as time went on most of us got the opportunity to get to know your son more and more personally.... Your son was one of the best, most motivated senior soldiers to help prepare us for what was coming. He was a mentor and a friend to everyone I can think of!"

Balm to grieving parents? Maybe, but he didn't have to write. He'd already sent a sympathy card and plant, which Heather has nourished to this day. Francis would grumble about "kids" who started out for long treks in the Afghan mountains in dirty socks or didn't take care of their equipment or whined or slowed the group down because they weren't in shape – behaviors that can cost lives in places like the Korengal.

Bobby Brandt was none of these. In Afghanistan, he and Francis and a soldier named Jon Demler paid the price for being good at what they did by catching some of the tougher assignments, which also led to a lasting friendship among them. Bobby described its beginnings in an email:

> During the deployment Frank, Demler and myself were always tasked with going the extra mile. We were not even in the same squad but were considered the most able to complete the more difficult missions. So

> in essence, we always got screwed together and we formed a really tight bond. I remember in the very beginning of our deployment on Operation Mountain Lion, I was assigned to go with Frank to clear a small house we came upon in the mountains. This was the first time they put us together and Frank said, 'Hell, yeah! I have the dream team.' That was the first time that I realized that he didn't hate me. He was just being hard on us at Fort Drum to prepare us for what he had already been through. After that operation we became really close friends. I will probably never be that close to anyone. It really is true that bonds formed through difficult times in war are special. Frank wasn't just a friend, he was a brother to me.

Soon afterwards, knowing Bobby's background in the restaurant business, Francis asked for advice on cooking schools. He wanted to become a chef when he got out of the Army.

"You're crazy," Bobby said. "Don't do it."

But Francis was determined. He loved cooking, and now they'd found something in common.

—m—

Their company – the 10th Mountain Division, 1st Battalion, 32nd Infantry Regiment, 2nd Platoon, Company C (or simply the 1-32, Combat Company) – receives brief mention in Sebastian Junger's book *War*, which traces the story of the National Guard unit that replaced them in 2007 in the notorious Korengal Valley. (The *corngall*, Francis would say.) Combat Company built the for-

Losing Francis

ward operating base (FOB) and several outposts occupied by the Guard soldiers Junger embedded with. He describes the Korengal Outpost as "a cheerless collection of bunkers and C-wire and bee huts that stretched several hundred yards up a steep hillside toward a band of holly trees that had been shredded by gunfire."[1]

Francis wrote to us from the Korengal on a postcard torn from an MRE food carton, dated May 18, 2006, about eighteen months before Junger arrived:

> Hey Family,
> I'm writing from the top of some nameless mountain which we are currently attempting to convert into an FOB. Sucks being the first guys here. We don't have much right now, but it gets better every day. We are the first U.S. forces to integrate a base camp with the Afghan Army. Needless to say, lots of top brass has been around lately, and reporters .... [M]y platoon will be a part of history, so to speak .... I will call when I can, don't worry about me. I love you.
>
> Francis D. Sommer
>
> P.S. I have a huge beard and haven't showered since April.
> P.P.S. MRE postcards suck.

He scribbled in the margins to make the pen write on the plasti-coated card. He wrote "I love you," rather than signing off "Love," as he usually did, and also signed his full name, probably to be sure someone other than us would know who wrote the card – hints of how grave conditions really were.

---

1 Sebastian Junger, *War* (New York: Twelve Books, 2010), p. 10.

We Were Goats

—⚜—

This region in Kunar Province was known to be the most dangerous place in Afghanistan. Americans occupied a number of sparsely-manned outposts on remote hilltops. Skirmishes occurred almost daily. Sometimes these amounted to brief machine gun bursts across the wide valleys, and sometimes they turned into brutal engagements that required air support and mortar fire delivered from distant bases. Occupying the Korengal had cost more than four dozen American lives by the time 10th Mountain left the region, and many more Afghan lives, both civilian and Afghan National Army soldiers. Sadly – one could say ironically, if the costs weren't so tragic – it turned out to be all for nothing, as U.S. forces were quietly withdrawn in 2010, after five years in the Korengal. Nothing gained and much lost.

The deployment was brutal. Missions at these isolated outposts could last months, and conditions were grim. Bobby dropped his voice into the key of utter frankness and described sharing a latrine with Francis: "We took a shit so close to each other that our knees bumped." Food and equipment were always in short supply because it was dangerous for helicopters to fly into the region. "But not too dangerous for us to be out there," Bobby said wryly. We heard the same from Francis in a November 2006 email describing a recent mission and hitting a characteristically sarcastic note:

> We were out about a week total, partly due to how long it took to reach the village, and partly because of the difficulty of getting a helicopter ride back. (The walk up was bad enough, and we didn't want to chance being ambushed on the way back down.) I feel like the aviation elements over here have really let us down this deployment. Moving in the mountains is no joke, and nothing raises morale like hearing that the birds won't come because they are afraid of being shot down. Like we are in a better position. However, the mission turned out good – we found a Russian heavy machine gun hidden near the village.

Combat Company took casualties on that tour, and Francis later told me he was concerned about the fitness of the unit replacing them. Altitude is a great equalizer, even among the fittest, and 10th Mountain soldiers knew that the new arrivals hadn't acclimated. Junger describes them taking the Guard troops on an orientation mission and running them up and down hillsides and mountain trails, where peaks could reach 10,000 feet or more. "Tenth Mountain was intentionally trying to break them off," Junger morosely observes, even hinting that they needlessly put the new guys in danger, as shots were fired at one point, the first time most of the Guard troops had ever been under fire.[2] Francis laughed when he read this scene. Like many full-time, active-duty soldiers, he didn't have a high opinion of the National Guard. He described a mission with these same troops in a March 2007 email:

---

2 Junger, p. 11.

> Sorry it has been so long but we were sent away for a bit. Not a fun mission, but only because we were attached to a Guard unit without a clue. These guys have been out so few times that they couldn't even remember how to get to the front gate of their own FOB when we returned.

When I mentioned the mountain trail episode to Bobby, as we drove to his house in Slidell after lunch, he grinned.

"We were goats."

Disappointingly, all Junger could say about Combat Company at the end of their tour was to describe them as "messed up."[3] They'd been out there for sixteen months, gone through some ferocious encounters, endured losses, sparse conditions, and the disappointment of having their deployment extended by more than four months, but they weren't so messed up that they couldn't run the Guard troops ragged.

Packs and equipment typically ran to eighty pounds. Bobby weighed himself before and after loading up for one mission and found he was carrying 140. He now lives with knee and back problems and has to sleep on his back on a hard surface. Like Francis, he also suffers from tinnitus, which he describes as an unending drone of cicadas buzzing in trees.

"I used to like cicadas," he said. "Now I can't stand them."

He also shared a perspective on the war in Afghanistan that in some instinctive way we even felt at home: a persistent undercurrent of low-voltage fear that seldom found expression but was part of our every day. Bobby contrasted his grandfather's experience in

3 Ibid.

World War II with his own in Afghanistan. Combat then sometimes meant weeks and even months of down time in or near bases, followed by big battles with massive casualties, and then more down time. But in Afghanistan, especially in the eastern mountains, "we were always alert," Bobby said, "always potentially under attack." There was no down time, especially at remote and vulnerable mountaintop outposts occupied by only a few soldiers that took hours to reach on foot with heavy packs.

Choppy waves drum a steady backbeat against the bow as we skim the surface of Lake Pontchartrain, a flat skipping stone with a propeller. Water splashes up. The wind whips my hat brim back like the trail cook's in an old-time Western. Only my chin strap keeps it from flying off into the waves. I'm in the forward seat – Bobby'd advised me not to sit on the gunwale just before he opened up the outboard – and behind me is Matthew, observant, smiling whenever I turn his way, while his father stands in back, one hand on the throttle, wearing sunglasses, his cap turned backwards, wind-blown, a cover guy for an outdoor sports magazine.

Ahead of us, above the horizon, a system of cumulus clouds shapes and reshapes itself in complex ways. Off the port side, several hundred yards distant, waterfront homes escalate in size and value as we gain distance from the canal and rows of stilted fishing camps where Bobby and his family live. A few of these mansions, he tells me, belong to professional athletes. Real estate

We Were Goats

soon gives way to marsh as we pass into the Pearl River Wildlife Management Area, a 35,000 acre reserve where Bobby hunts duck and fishes. I face forward on the open water, letting wind and spray shower me. Welcoming it. Conversation is clipped, more pointing than words. We can't hear well over the motor and the wind. Besides, it's too fine a moment to do anything but lose ourselves in it. And too, I don't want to betray that my face is wet with tears.

I am, at this moment, Francis. Not his father, not his proxy. I am him. He is here having the day he was supposed to have only weeks after he was gone. He'd planned to be here, to take the trip I'm taking now, over three years later, to get out on the water with Bobby and Matthew, to let wind and spray and this wildlife-rich marshland purge the demons of war and the demons of returning home. Like many who fought in these wars, he found life more complicated here. It may have been hell there, but it was simple – you knew what to do. Each task linear, the goals clear: do a thing (build something, go somewhere with half your body weight packed on your back; hustle here, fight; hustle there, fight; return to your post, eat, clean your weapon, shit, doze but never sleep), survive and get the fuck out and make sure everyone you came with also got the fuck out. But here at home there was no war – America was not at war; it was at the mall. He'd sneer at the sight of shiny Hummers taking up a whole lane, drifting this way and that while the driver yammered on a cell phone. A Hummer to transport a few bags of groceries and a new pair of shoes back home through treacherous suburban roads – a statement, solidarity: *Support the troops!* There's the yellow-ribbon magnet on the gleaming bumper. "He goin' on a mission?" Francis would quip. Well, yes, shopping. A mission. *Supporting the troops!*

This is the deep structure, where our sensibilities mingle, where memory is a flood tide washing into the present, like the backwash of salt water flowing into the canal behind Bobby's place, infusing fresh water flowing downstream. These hours alone have justified my travel from Kansas to Louisiana, my visit to Bobby and his family. This is, I think, what Bobby wants me to see, what he would have shown Francis.

We have slowed to a cruising speed. Bobby steers into the labyrinth of canals that weave through the Pearl River marshes. It's safe to stand, easy to talk. The wind is buffered by the surrounding tallgrass. Matthew names the birds – egrets, pelicans, an eagle perched on a dead tree. His acquaintance with wildlife is impressive for a six-year-old – for an any-year-old. He spends a lot of time out here with his father. I give him my camera and he takes pictures of a shrimp boat with its nets widely spread, suspended over the water like a giant pterodactyl's spiny wings. The boat swarms with gulls as it passes. Bobby motors through canals where he hunts duck. His and Allison's grocery bills are nominal because of all the fish and game he brings home. He describes a hunting trip with a couple of Army friends he's planned for next fall, after he graduates from law school – deep into the New Mexico mountains, hunting elk, traveling lightly with small packs, the very least they'll need to camp, oh yes, so much less than they lugged overseas. I recall the final scene in *The Deer Hunter,* Robert De Niro's serenity as he sites the buck, but I have no doubt Bobby *will* pull the trigger. I don't mention the reference – "That reminds me of …" – a sure way to undercut his story, one of those phrases that usurps ownership, diminishes the storyteller. His hunting trip, I come to realize, as he returns to it over the next couple of days, is more than a breather after law school; it is when he'll complete his passage from there to here. He carries grief too, for Francis, for others, and injuries, and also guilt – a mission he didn't go on, another soldier's death. He'd plunged back into life after his second tour in Afghanistan – work, family, school, financial challenges. He'll breathe mountain air and track game, a linear task in a place where no one shoots back. Francis would have gone on this trip. I'm here to imagine that for him, too. The images come easily as Bobby describes his plans. I would not have understood without being here.

Bobby is making his own recipe for gumbo while Allison feeds Elizabeth and I play Mousetrap with Matthew. I haven't played Mousetrap since Francis and his brother and sister were children. In all the years since it was first released when I was a kid, it hasn't changed. Francis liked board games. Regrets simmer from those nights when I was too tired or lazy to play. I'm soon absorbed in making the mousetrap work. We finish the game and Matthew wants to play again, so we do. And again. And when there's no game, we just build the mousetrap and set it in motion. Matthew finally wears me out and carries on by himself.

Bobby and Allison chat openly about everything – money, politics, family stuff. They laugh easily together. After dinner, they debate whether women should serve in the infantry (both against) and the merits of a woman becoming president. Bobby's okay with a woman in the White House (though probably not Hillary), Allison not at all. "Women are too emotional," she says. Conversation is frank and yet floats lightly on the surface of divisive issues. I remain aloof, more amused at their exchange than drawn into the debate. Allison is even more conservative than Bobby. Before the weekend's out, I watch a video of her firing a 9mm. handgun at a blown-out TV.

The gumbo is the best I've ever tasted. Bobby'd promised to make it for Francis, and here I am to eat it.

"It's so weird to hear you call him Francis," he says. "He was just Frank or Sarnt Sommer."

I share our trials with the name – mostly Francis's. It's a common name in the Northeast, where Heather and I grew up and we lived until he was five. Not so much in the Midwest. It made him a target in school and was perpetually misspelled as *Frances*. Even some adults made him feel weird about his name. Later in high school, he was so tired of it that we offered him the choice to use his middle name, David, or even have his name legally changed.

Or if you want, we said, we'll just call you Frank.

"That'd be weird," he said. We should call him Francis. "What else would you call me?"

We Were Goats

A storm blows in on Sunday. We won't be going out on the water again. Bobby has reading to do for school, and I want to catch up on email. Country music videos play on the big screen, and Allison fixes a bottle for Little-bit. Matthew is bored and restless. He hovers around me, first one side, then the other, sneaking up on me along the sofa, sidling in until he's at my shoulder. Allison calls him away but soon he's back. Finally I cave. We build another mousetrap. Soon we're all playing again, building, laughing, circling the cheese. But the storm is gaining strength, blowing in fiercely across the marsh and up the canal. Clouds moil darkly over the city on the horizon. A sharp gust blows a section of flashing loose over the porch. It swings dangerously and threatens the living room windows.

Bobby realizes he has to do something about it. The porch is about twelve feet over the lower deck. The flashing swings across the railing in a clumsy pendulum-like motion. Hammer in hand, Bobby leaps onto the railing. The thing fights him as he nails it in place. He's indifferent to the height. Not foolish, but agile, focused. Watching him, I can see why he and Francis did well together in Afghanistan. He's not someone you need to explain a task to, or wonder if he'll be able to do it. He can see the end of a task and the way through it at a glance. Caution is a matter of doing it right, and knowing your limits. He knows that gravity will win if he doesn't respect it.

Later, inside, with the children settled for naps, I share photos on my laptop of Francis's life in Kansas. I've brought several items, too, including the funeral service program and Francis's Kansas City Chiefs ball cap. Worn and sweat-stained, it wouldn't have fetched a dollar on eBay, but small things matter – tokens, signs. Gateways to memory. They touch our senses, launch images from the past. Bobby is a Saints fan. He and Francis loved the rivalry. I'm still chattering and looking at the cap and don't realize that beside me they've both collapsed into tears. This moment turns out to be, after all, the service Bobby couldn't attend – the time we spent then at our kitchen table, telling stories, looking at pictures, weeping, and laughing too.

Bobby grins and promises to root for the Chiefs – when they're not playing the Saints. Allison shares a story about Frank's last visit. They were blowing off fireworks one night at Bobby's hunting cabin on a remote parcel of bayou, tossing Black Cats one at a time into the campfire. Allison threw in a bundle of a half dozen or more, but it landed off to the side without igniting. She forgot about it – until later, when the Black Cats exploded and sent Francis and Bobby leaping for cover. She's laughing so hard she can barely sputter through the story. Bobby nods dryly, recalling how he and Francis instinctively hit the deck, dodging a sudden burst of Taliban bullets in the dark Louisiana forest that surrounded them.

—⚜—

There was one thing I wanted to ask Bobby. This was the right time. It was about Shudergay.

Combat Company had engaged in two serious firefights at Shudergay, a hamlet in the Afghan mountains that border Pakistan. This was the home of a Taliban leader named Habib Jan, who had murdered many of his own countrymen and inspired fear in villages throughout the region. He was known to have ordered the beheading of his own brother.

The first battle at Shudergay took place while Francis was on leave in July 2006. He was angry about being ordered to take leave only four months into the tour, and then, while he was enjoying the nightlife and beaches of Barcelona, two men from his company were killed. That was the news that greeted him on his return.

According to company commander Capt. Robert Stanton, the mission to get Habib Jan had become personal. "This guy was responsible for the only two soldiers I lost," he said, following the second battle at Shudergay, which resulted in Habib Jan's death. "The extension was almost worth it to get rid of him. No, I would say it was definitely worth it."[4]

In April 2007, Combat Company was ordered to revisit Shudergay, where it was thought Taliban fighters were using the now-deserted village to regroup. The climb alone is difficult, on foot over rocky exposed goat trails, with heavy packs and weaponry, to an elevation of over 8,000 feet.

Two book-length accounts of Shudergay have been published by a writer named James Christ (pronounced like fist), *Shudergay* and *The 17 Hour Firefight*. The former details the first encounter, while Francis was on leave in 2006, and in the second, the following year, both he and Bobby are mentioned a number of times. The only other written accounts rely wholly on official Army sources.

---

4 Kevin Dougherty, "Firefight kills hunted Afghan militant," *Stars and Stripes*, Mideast edition, May 22, 2007.

Christ's books are based mostly on interviews with soldiers who went on these missions and include exhaustive lists of ordnance, acronyms, and photos. Yet it's plain that editorial attention is lacking. Typographical and grammatical errors recur frequently enough to become distracting. Acronyms litter the pages in confusing ways – even humorously, if unintentionally so: "He had been on his way to the TOC when the explosion of gunfire erupted atop the mountain. Salmon didn't need anyone to tell him there was a TIC. He ran to the TOC and saw everyone in Combat Main scrambling into motion to get ready to enter a fight."[5] The book's title appears on the front cover as *The 17 Hour Firefight* and then on the title page as *The Seventeen-Hour Firefight*. The printed text on the back cover is rendered illegible in a photo whose shadows consume it.

These books appear to be self-published – not itself a reason for criticism, as the market for them is likely to be limited. And they do perform a service in attempting to document events that might otherwise be neglected in the long and tangled history of this war. Christ deserves credit for bringing attention to these encounters and making the effort to record them. But the obvious haste and even sloppiness of their production have the unfortunate result of casting doubt on their reliability.

That's what I wanted to ask Bobby on that stormy afternoon: How accurate was this account?

He shook his head and snorted as I pulled a dog-eared, scribbled, post-it bookmarked copy of *The 17 Hour Firefight* out of my

---

5 James F. Christ, *The 17 Hour Firefight: C/1/32 at Shudergay*, April 22, 2007 (N.P., 2012), p. 30.

bag. He said the book made him so angry he couldn't finish reading it. He pointed to the cover photo, which he'd taken, though he wasn't given credit. And the photo itself is misleading. It wasn't even from the Shudergay mission. "There's no way we'd have been standing around like that, without helmets or armor, on that mission," he said. He leafed through the book and waved a finger over several more of his photos that were credited to another soldier.

He snorted again in disgust. His own fault. Christ had called to interview him, but Bobby didn't know him and wasn't interested in talking. It seemed like the book was about to be published, he added. He felt pressured by the author, which only made him more resistant to talk. He just wanted to leave this battle and the whole deployment behind him. Not an uncommon sentiment. Francis's former squad leader and close friend, Staff Sgt. Chris Bryant, who'd been in both the 2006 and 2007 Shudergay battles, responded similarly when I asked him about these books. He'd been interviewed, he told me, but hadn't even read the books. "I try to live my life as far as possible not thinking about overseas," Bryant said in an email. "The only reason I did the interview for the guy is so that maybe another unit could learn from it."

After reading *Shudergay*, about the first battle in this village while Francis was on leave, I decided to talk to Christ. He wasn't easy to find because the publisher, Battlefield Publishing, lists no website, address, email, or phone number. (The second book doesn't even name a publisher.) I finally located him through a talk-radio host who'd interviewed him, and we subsequently spoke on the phone. That was when I learned he'd written *The*

17 Hour Firefight, about the second Shudergay battle, on April 22, 2007, in which Bobby and Francis participated.

Christ told me, with some enthusiasm, that Francis gave the order that launched this battle, a scene described in the book's early pages. He was on point as 2nd Platoon approached the village, when an Afghan man was spotted on the hillside. The soldiers assumed he was a lookout. Francis shouted in Pashto for the man to raise his hands, but he backed away and when Francis called again, he turned and ran. According to Christ, moments later the man pulled a rifle from behind a rock and Francis shouted, "Light him up!"

"Almost everyone had been sighting in on the man," Christ wrote in *The 17 Hour Firefight*. "The insurgent died in an uphill rain of bullets."[6]

Christ seemed to get a charge out of describing this scene to me on the phone. In fact, there'd been some telephone-tag before we finally connected and he'd even mentioned it in a voicemail.

"Light him up!"

What I was thinking when I read this scene in the book: *Francis speaks Pashto?!*

Probably not fluent, but using the language in a tense moment like that suggests some confidence with it. My son was learning a Middle Eastern language.

Christ's tone bothered me, both on the phone and in his writing – his fervor, his eagerness. They *lit* this man up. Francis led the charge. It sound more like a football game than war. This pitch pervades his books. More so than any typographical, punctuation,

---

6 Ibid., p. 13.

grammatical, or even factual errors (and there are many of each in both books), Christ's enthusiasm and bias (and biblical quotes) detract from the credibility of the work. Insurgent leaders have "henchmen"; "Combat Company was always big on mortars and 240B machineguns [sic]"; "... they are among the rare few, in a small fraternity of men, who can call themselves warriors."[7] This is the language of recruitment ads and Rambo movies. Unreliable as either history or journalism, Christ's books pay homage to these soldiers through a seemingly detailed, yet uncritical and unverified, account of the Shudergay missions.

Bobby's discomfort was much like mine – and he'd been there. Whatever it was that made them "light up" another man, if that's happened, had happened there, and that's where he wanted to stay. And I already knew how much Francis detested the hoorah, chest-thumping spirit that infused the way some (usually civilians) described combat and the military in general.

Once they entered the village, 2nd Platoon quickly found itself trapped. "Every position we had, we were pinned down," Bryant later told a reporter for *Stars and Stripes*.[8] More than forty Taliban fighters occupied high ground on a surrounding ridge, with reinforcements on the way. A sniper was trying to pick off individuals, nearly hitting Francis twice and sending another shot between Bobby's legs. Bobby sketched the terrain inside the back cover of my book and described the demanding climb a detachment from Combat Company's 3rd Platoon was making to the west of the village to engage fighters who were descending from

7 Ibid., pp, 145, 3, 152.
8 Dougherty.

that direction. There's little doubt 2nd Platoon, which was running low on ammunition, would have been overrun had it not been for this group's effort.

"I give them all the credit," Bobby said. "They really had to hump it to get up there."

Official Army reportage and incidental accounts like Christ's two books – and the stories soldiers themselves tell months and even years after the engagement – offer most of what we see inside this seemingly endless war. Embedded reporters and writers, like Sebastian Junger and his partner, the late Tim Heatherington, offer some of the few glimpses we have of battles like this, but even these are only glimpses into a vast, now decades-long conflict. The war in Afghanistan is not being documented as, say, Vietnam was, which left a rich literature of battlefield reporting. Ezra Pound famously said, "Fundamental accuracy of statement is the sole morality of writing." Poor editing, failing to verify the provenance of photos and accurately credit them, and sub-standard production values undercut the authenticity of Christ's accounts of Shudergay, battles that reveal much about the nature of this war, its diasporic character, the elusiveness of the enemy, who can fade into villages and escape over borders, and the ambiguous purpose and meaning of the war itself. Bobby also reminded me that Christ relied mostly on what the men who were interviewed told him – and, he added, that a few may have selectively padded their own roles.

When the 2nd Platoon soldiers finally descended the mountain hours after this exhausting firefight, they were greeted by an order to turn around and climb back to the village. The final battlefield assessment still needed to be taken, and they had to do it. The reaction was swift and bitter, and from a few loud, but they returned and finished the task. A number of silver and bronze stars were awarded for this mission. Staff Sgt. Chris Bryant received his second silver star; his first had been for the earlier Shudergay battle.

For Francis the epilogue was bittersweet – and it is for us too, though in a different way. Here's the unvarnished email he wrote soon afterwards:

> From: Frank Sommer
> Sent: Wednesday, May 23, 2007 8:42 AM
> To: Robert Sommer
> Subject: Re: Stars and Stripes
>
> Yeah, that was the thing I was telling you about. It lifted our spirits almost as much as getting redeployment dates. Unfortunately, I won't be getting any award for that because my squad leader is a lazy piece of shit. He didn't feel like writing up any awards. I sure do miss having Chris [Bryant] as squad leader. I put all of my guys in for Army Commendation medals with Valor devices.
>
> I'm looking forward, as well – the word is still that we should be home around the twelfth! I'll call once we are at JAF [Jalalabad Air Field]. Talk to you then.
> Love, Francis

He told me later that the squad leader, whom I won't name here, didn't write up anyone for an award because he didn't want to be bothered with the paperwork.

Losing Francis

It angered me at the time, as it would any parent, I suppose. The recognition doesn't matter now – that was for Francis, not for Heather and me – but knowing that he took care of his men does, that does matter. Knowing he did that much is enough.

"Dear Friends," wrote Clovis and Benny Martin in 1929 to streetcar union members who'd gone on strike in New Orleans, "We are with you heart and Soule, at any time you .,are around the French Market, don't forget to drop in at Martin's Coffee Stand & Restaurant, Cor. Ursuline & North Peters Sts., our meal is free to any members of Division 194" [*sic passim*]. The free meals for these "poor boys," as the Martins called them, were hefty sandwiches on oversized bread loafs special ordered from the bakery just for the strikers. The Martin brothers later dubbed the sandwiches "po' boys," which have long since become a hallmark of New Orleans fare. I'd been told I had to have one.

Bobby ordered the same. They were so big that the little appetite I had shriveled when mine landed in front of me. The sandwiches mostly sat in our baskets while we talked.

Bobby had encouraged to Francis to come here and settle with him, at least for a while. He knew Francis was in trouble, that he couldn't sleep and carried guilt and unthinkable memories from incidents on his tours; that he was drinking too much, though Bobby didn't know how much. He's not much of a drinker himself. Life here, he thought, with less booze and more time outdoors, and with his family, would be good for Frank.

He'd molt the sorrow and guilt that encrusted him.

He may have been right too – Heather and I think he was – but I've also wondered if Francis might have just brought his troubles with him. With children in the house, with Bobby in school, there'd have to be limits. And Bobby didn't know how bad things had gotten; that Frank had put himself through six-weeks of painful, in-patient rehab at the Kansas City VA Medical Center. He'd withdrawn from school and gotten a leave from his job so he could go into the program. He was released just days before he was to stand as best man at his brother's wedding. Only Heather and I knew how fragile he was, how terrified; how I had to go outside with him that evening, just the two of us on the dark street, so he could pull himself together long enough to sit through dinner. This was only five months before we lost him.

Alcoholism is a cursed disease, at once both sickness and cure for many veterans. "Liquor was medicine for the anger that made them hurt, for the pain of loss," writes Leslie Marmon Silko in her novel *Ceremony*, "medicine for tight bellies and choked up throats." Francis fought his way through his brother's wedding day. I don't believe he fought more courageously at Shudergay.

I shared this with Bobby. This and other stories. We'd only known each other for an hour. We nibbled at our sandwiches. He told me what Frank had done for him and Allison on Bobby's second deployment to Afghanistan. She was terrified while he was gone. After the first tour, they knew how bad it was there. We'd all – Heather and I too – seen reports of losses coming back in the stark, formulaic prose of Army press releases. ("Two 10th

Mountain Division Soldiers were killed in the Pech River Valley, Afghanistan ... when their vehicle was struck by an improvised explosive device.") We'd gone through the long blackouts while they were in the mountains. Allison would call Frank in the middle of the night, or at his job, or when he was in class. He always got right back to her, she said. Even in class he'd send a text to say he'd call shortly. Not hearing from (or about) Bobby, he told her, was good. He knew the conditions, what they'd be doing. He would talk her through. She called him "her rock." They were grateful – still were, both Bobby and Allison. Their hospitality to me was without doubt partly an expression of gratitude for what he did for them then.

Bobby's eyes were wet. We both leaned on our elbows, hands folded, the un-eaten food between us. "I think about him every day," he said. "I just miss him."

My fears from an hour earlier were gone like the plane's smoky contrails. It would be all right. We brought the leftover po' boys home to Allison. I met the children. Bobby and Matthew and I went out on the water the following morning. I wasn't here for me. I was here for Francis.

Epilogue

> *All I have is a voice*
> *To undo the folded lie*
> —W.H. Auden, "September 1, 1939"

TENSE SHIFTS. SHIFTED. WILL SHIFT.

This is the future.
Now.
It was.
That was the future then, too.
But this is the time I feared.
When grief is no longer all-consuming.
When the past recedes and pulls its present-ness away.
When, as Robert Penn Warren writes,

> *sometimes a face, as though from air,*
> *Will stare at you with a boyish smile – but, not*
> *Stone-moored, blows away like dandelion fuzz.*[1]

---

1 Robert Penn Warren, *Rumor Verified: Poems 1979-198*0 (New York: Random

I feared it becoming easier.

Not as betrayal.

Rather because I'd have let go, and I would forget things.

The stories to tell to those who came later – like the nieces he'll never know who just emerged into life this past year. Nor would others, as Time passes/d.

It's now over six years.

Warren's poems often wander in the ether of Time. His lines are from "Small Eternity," which I asked Francis's godfather, Dave Christi (whose name Francis David carried), to read at the funeral.

Even then, days after we lost him, I sensed how the future would bend my grief.

And this too: that banalities would diminish it by their very banality.

Like the time I went into a bathroom to weep and found the toilet stopped up and ended up putting tears aside to plunge the john.

Like that.

The folded lie.

How the wars slip into the past, or seem to, even as we continue to fight in Iraq and Afghanistan, and now in Yemen and Syria and, it seems, everywhere. But still Iraq and Afghanistan, because oddly, in some weird perversion of time, we collectively think of those wars as if they were already in the past. Now fixed there. Events that began and ended.

House, 1981), p. 19.

Epilogue

Americans mostly seem little interested in history, except as it's portrayed in the mythologies we embrace, or the Hollywood versions of same: Mel Gibson as *The Patriot,* John Wayne in [*Name Your American War*], Mel Gibson (again) in *Vietnam* (John Wayne was there, too – even though he wasn't), George C. Scott as *Patton*, Lee Marvin and his misfits kill a lot of snooty Germans, Alec Guinness builds a bridge. Rambo takes Afghanistan.

So forth.

How we know war, which for more than a century has always been somewhere else. So what is it we think we know?

And what of the people whose countries we invade?

War nourishes our sense of greatness and the greatness of our democracy – and of capitalism, and the inherent goodness of America, and its exceptional nature.

Folded and refolded, like bread dough.

The baked product is warm and rich and digestible.

But man cannot live by …

Francis discovered the music of the 60s and 70s on his own. In Iraq he asked us to send CDs: Neil Young, Crosby, Stills and Nash, Eric Clapton, The Allman Brothers. He liked *Eat a Peach.* "Mountain Jam" was soothing. He knew "Blue Sky" was my favorite tune. It'd been all rap and punk all the time in high school, but something changed in Iraq. I don't know what or how. But this was his music now. His computer was loaded with tunes from that era. As I mentioned in "Leavenworth," he was listening to "Here Comes the Sun" when he crashed.

When he left the Army, he listened to a lot of Neil Young and gave me a couple of his newer CDs. I still had Neil Young and CSN LPs from back in the day. But Francis wasn't giving them to me because I liked this music, but because *he* liked it, he'd discovered it, it spoke to him, he wanted to share it. It was new to him. Its oldness to me was irrelevant. And, as Ezra Pound might have said, Young kept making it new, writing songs about the environment, war, the injustices and indignities suffered by Native Americans, the loss of wild places, how the wind on the prairie fills your spirit in ways nothing else can.

Our tragedy wouldn't nudge the meter on the scale of environmental, cultural, and human devastation brought down by these wars and now playing out in refugee crises across the Mediterranean and Sub-Saharan Africa and beyond – all made worse, too, by global climate disruption. This tragedy is compounded by the infinite number of squandered opportunities of these years, leaving us only to imagine what might have been if resources plowed into war had been devoted to education and renewable energy and healthcare, domestically and globally. Nearly $5 trillion wasted. Thousands of American lives. Millions of people killed, injured, made homeless, impoverished. And many of the survivors – including many who assisted our troops in Iraq and Afghanistan – now rejected as refugees in the U.S.

Epilogue

Part of the myth we've collectively embraced, if not for this global chaos at least for these wars, is to blame the Bush and Obama administrations. I understand that perspective and have especially not spared Bush and his cohorts in the previous pages, but folding in that lie is one of the ways we absolve ourselves of complicity. The Iraq War began with a lie – with many lies – but how we see those lies now is also false. That is, Bush is not to blame for the war, or even the lies. We are. We knew they were lies. It took longer for some than for others to figure it out, but we knew. We looked away – either by consuming the folded lies or ignoring them, as we do with the global environmental crisis, the inhumane labor conditions that deliver cheap goods and clothing to our stores, the abominable human rights track records of countries that sell us oil and other commodities, and finally our pure consumption and reckless waste.

Here's another lie: All soldiers are heroes.

And another: "Thank you for your service."

And another: We take care of our veterans.

Francis (and a lot of others) didn't (don't) want to hear it.

And we've fallen way short on the last.

In his novel *All the King's Men*, Warren writes, "… we shall go out of the house and into the convulsion of the world, out of history into history and the awful responsibility of Time."[2]

---

2 Robert Penn Warren, *All the King's Men* (New York: Harcourt Brace, 1945; Bantam rpt., 1974), p. 438.

We are makers of history in whatever ways we participate.

Participation is not optional.

Ignoring the wars and their victims, failing to care for the planet, choosing to avoid or face what disturbs us, to act or not to act – history absorbs every action or inaction.

That's the default setting.

Francis remains with us – my son, Heather's son, our children's brother, the uncle of their infant children, who will come to know him in a special and separate way from others who surround them now.

And in time, we will all slip into history.

Francis David Sommer
May 12, 1983 – February 11, 2011

Acknowledgments

Several people generously read all or parts of the manuscript at various stages and offered suggestions to improve it. Susan Rieke, S.C.L., and Steve Physioc gave it thorough readings that were at once sympathetic yet not wanting for detailed and critical suggestions to improve it. David and Judy Ray read several essays prior to their appearance in literary journals and found soft spots I would have regretted discovering once they were published. Elizabeth Witte, Associate Editor of *The Common Online*; Kara Cochran, Managing Editor of *Rathalla Review*; and Lindsey DeLoach Jones, Editor of *Emrys Journal*, offered incisive guidance to sharpen the essays that appeared in their respective journals. Marc Estrin, editor and co-publisher of Fomite Press, found the fault lines in an earlier version of the manuscript and pressed me into narrative space I'd consciously or unconsciously avoided because it was too uncomfortable to go there. Donna Bister, production editor and co-publisher of Fomite, prepared the manuscript with skill and patience. Any and all lapses, factual and otherwise, are mine, as are those opinions and observations I've made to which not all may subscribe.

Among the many soldiers with whom Francis served, several have remained friends to our family and were helpful in developing this book. Matt McKenzie responded promptly and informatively to my questions about the Iraq and Afghanistan deployments. Chris Bryant shared stories about himself and Francis with a welcome and refreshing candor. Isaac Nam offered inspiration in ways he can't really know. Bobby Brandt and his family opened their doors and their hearts to me and shared more stories and details than I could possibly include in this volume.

Melissa Jacobson and Monique Peña at the Kansas City VA Medical Center Voluntary Services Unit have taken great personal interest in The Francis D. Sommer Memorial Fund for Homeless Veterans since its inception and worked diligently to put donations to work efficiently and with thoughtful oversight. My entire family is grateful to them, as we also are to the hundreds of people who have contributed to this fund and continue to do so.

David Ray once told me in a darkly understated way that we both "belong to a club we'd rather not have joined" – that of parents who have lost children. Each parent has a story. Each has been hollowed out in ways that others may never know (and hopefully never will). We have met many such parents, and more than a few have befriended us through this common tragedy. I wanted at least the space of one paragraph to acknowledge the ways all of the parents we've known who have lost children – and many others we've never met and never will – have contributed to the impetus for this book.

Finally, without the support and encouragement and sometimes sheer tolerance of my family I would not have conceived or completed this project. Some – much – of what I've written has been painful for them to read and relive. I see this work finally as a shared project, unimaginable in conception or meaning without Erin and Alex and my life partner and closest friend and soulmate Heather as participants in not only the narrative but the creation of the work itself.

About the Author

Robert F. Sommer is the author of two novels, *Where the Wind Blew* (Wessex 2008) and *A Great Fullness* (Fomite 2016). His essays and stories have appeared in many literary and scholarly journals. Bob is a lecturer at the University of Saint Mary, Leavenworth, and works for the Sierra Club's Kansas Chapter in support of its mission to explore, enjoy, and protect the planet.

Fomite

About Fomite

A fomite is a medium capable of transmitting infectious organisms from one individual to another.

"The activity of art is based on the capacity of people to be infected by the feelings of others." Tolstoy, *What Is Art?*

Writing a review on Amazon, Good Reads, Shelfari, Library Thing or other social media sites for readers will help the progress of independent publishing. To submit a review, go to the book page on any of the sites and follow the links for reviews. Books from independent presses rely on reader to reader communications.

For more information or to order any of our books, visit
http://www.fomitepress.com/FOMITE/Our_Books.html

More Titles from Fomite...

Novels
Joshua Amses — *During This, Our Nadir*
Joshua Amses — *Raven or Crow*
Joshua Amses — *The Moment Before an Injury*
Jaysinh Birjepatel — *The Good Muslim of Jackson Heights*
Jaysinh Birjepatel — *Nothing Beside Remains*
David Brizer — *Victor Rand*
Paula Closson Buck — *Summer on the Cold War Planet*
Dan Chodorkoff — *Loisaida*
David Adams Cleveland — *Time's Betrayal*
Jaimee Wriston Colbert — *Vanishing Acts*
Roger Coleman — *Skywreck Afternoons*
Marc Estrin — *Hyde*
Marc Estrin — *Kafka's Roach*

Fomite

Marc Estrin — *Speckled Vanities*
Zdravka Evtimova — *In the Town of Joy and Peace*
Zdravka Evtimova — *Sinfonia Bulgarica*
Daniel Forbes — *Derail This Train Wreck*
Greg Guma — *Dons of Time*
Richard Hawley — *The Three Lives of Jonathan Force*
Lamar Herrin — *Father Figure*
Michael Horner — *Damage Control*
Ron Jacobs — *All the Sinners Saints*
Ron Jacobs — *Short Order Frame Up*
Ron Jacobs — *The Co-conspirator's Tale*
Scott Archer Jones — *A Rising Tide of People Swept Away*
Julie Justicz — *A Boy Called Home*
Maggie Kast — *A Free Unsullied Land*
Darrell Kastin — *Shadowboxing with Bukowski*
Coleen Kearon — *Feminist on Fire*
Coleen Kearon — *#triggerwarning*
Jan English Leary — *Thicker Than Blood*
Diane Lefer — *Confessions of a Carnivore*
Rob Lenihan — *Born Speaking Lies*
Colin Mitchell — *Roadman*
Ilan Mochari — *Zinsky the Obscure*
Peter Nash — *Parsimony*
Peter Nash — *The Perfection of Things*
Gregory Papadoyiannis — *The Baby Jazz*
Andy Potok — *My Father's Keeper*
Kathryn Roberts — *Companion Plants*
Robert Rosenberg — *Isles of the Blind*
Fred Russell — *Rafi's World*
Ron Savage — *Voyeur in Tangier*
David Schein — *The Adoption*
Lynn Sloan — *Principles of Navigation*
L.E. Smith — *The Consequence of Gesture*
L.E. Smith — *Travers' Inferno*
L.E. Smith — *Untimely RIPped*
Bob Sommer — *A Great Fullness*

Fomite

Tom Walker — *A Day in the Life*
Susan V. Weiss — *My God, What Have We Done?*
Peter M. Wheelwright — *As It Is On Earth*
Suzie Wizowaty — *The Return of Jason Green*

Poetry

Anna Blackmer — *Hexagrams*
Antonello Borra — *Alfabestiario*
Antonello Borra — *AlphaBetaBestiaro*
David Cavanagh — *Cycling in Plato's Cave*
James Connolly — *Picking Up the Bodies*
Greg Delanty — *Loosestrife*
Mason Drukman — *Drawing on Life*
J. C. Ellefson — *Foreign Tales of Exemplum and Woe*
Tina Escaja — *Caida Libre/Free Fall*
Anna Faktorovich — *Improvisational Arguments*
Barry Goldensohn — *Snake in the Spine, Wolf in the Heart*
Barry Goldensohn — *The Hundred Yard Dash Man*
Barry Goldensohn — *The Listener Aspires to the Condition of Music*
R. L. Green — *When* — *You Remember Deir Yassin*
Kate Magill — *Roadworthy Creature, Roadworthy Craft*
Tony Magistrale — *Entanglements*
Andreas Nolte — *Mascha: The Poems of Mascha Kaléko*
Sherry Olson — *Four-Way Stop*
David Polk — *Drinking the River*
Janice Miller Potter — *Meanwell*
Joseph D. Reich — *Connecting the Dots to Shangrila*
Joseph D. Reich — *The Hole That Runs Through Utopia*
Joseph D. Reich — *The Housing Market*
Joseph D. Reich — *The Derivation of Cowboys and Indians*
Kenneth Rosen and Richard Wilson — *Gomorrah*
Fred Rosenblum — *Vietnumb*

Fomite

David Schein — *My Murder and Other Local News*
Harold Schweizer — *Miriam's Book*
Scott T. Starbuck — *Industrial Oz*
Scott T. Starbuck — *Hawk on Wire*
Seth Steinzor — *Among the Lost*
Seth Steinzor — *To Join the Lost*
Susan Thomas — *The Empty Notebook Interrogates Itself*
Susan Thomas — *In the Sadness Museum*
Paolo Valesio and Todd Portnowitz — *Midnight in Spoleto*
Sharon Webster — *Everyone Lives Here*
Tony Whedon — *The Tres Riches Heures*
Tony Whedon — *The Falkland Quartet*
Claire Zoghb — *Dispatches from Everest*

Stories
Jay Boyer — *Flight*
Michael Cocchiarale — *Still Time*
Michael Cocchiarale — *This Is Ware*
Neil Connelly — *In the Wake of Our Vows*
Catherine Zobal Dent — *Unfinished Stories of Girls*
Zdravka Evtimova —*Carts and Other Stories*
John Michael Flynn — *Off to the Next Wherever*
Derek Furr — *Semitones*
Derek Furr — *Suite for Three Voices*
Elizabeth Genovise — *Where There Are Two or More*
Andrei Guriuanu — *Body of Work*
Zeke Jarvis — *In A Family Way*
Jan English Leary — *Skating on the Vertical*
Marjorie Maddox — *What She Was Saying*
William Marquess — *Boom-shacka-lacka*
Gary Miller — *Museum of the Americas*
Jennifer Anne Moses — *Visiting Hours*
Martin Ott — *Interrogations*

Fomite

Jack Pulaski — *Love's Labours*
Charles Rafferty — *Saturday Night at Magellan's*
Ron Savage — *What We Do For Love*
Fred Skolnik — *Americans and Other Stories*
Lynn Sloan — *This Far Is Not Far Enough*
L.E. Smith — *Views Cost Extra*
Caitlin Hamilton Summie — *To Lay To Rest Our Ghosts*
Susan Thomas — *Among Angelic Orders*
Tom Walker — *Signed Confessions*
Silas Dent Zobal — *The Inconvenience of the Wings*

Odd Birds
Micheal Breiner — *the way none of this happened*
J. C. Ellefson — *Under the Influence*
David Ross Gunn — *Cautionary Chronicles*
Andrei Guriuanu — *The Darkest City*
Gail Holst-Warhaft — *The Fall of Athens*
Roger Leboitz — *A Guide to the Western Slopes and the Outlying Area*
dug Nap — *Artsy Fartsy*
Delia Bell Robinson — *A Shirtwaist Story*
Peter Schumann — *Bread & Sentences*
Peter Schumann — *Charlotte Salomon*
Peter Schumann — *Faust 3*
Peter Schumann — *Planet Kasper, Volumes One and Two*
Peter Schumann — *We*

Plays
Stephen Goldberg — *Screwed and Other Plays*
Michele Markarian — *Unborn Children of America*

Essays
Robert Sommer — *Losing Francis*

www.ingramcontent.com/pod-product-compliance
Lightning Source LLC
Chambersburg PA
CBHW021430080526
44588CB00009B/483